God Gave the
INCREASE

© 2015 by TGS International, a wholly owned subsidiary of Christian Aid Ministries, Berlin, Ohio.

All rights reserved. No part of this book may be used, reproduced, or stored in any retrieval system, in any form or by any means, electronic or mechanical, without written permission from the publisher except for brief quotations embodied in critical articles and reviews.

ISBN: 978-1-941213-59-9
Cover design and layout: Teresa Sommers
Printed in the USA

Published by:
TGS International
P.O. Box 355
Berlin, Ohio 44610 USA
Phone: 330-893-4828
Fax: 330-893-2305
www.tgsinternational.com

TGS000994

God Gave the
INCREASE

ROBERT STAUFFER

TABLE OF CONTENTS

Introduction VII

Prologue X

Time line of major events in MIC's work in the North XVII

PART ONE: THE WORK BEGINS

1. In the Beginning 21
2. Exodus from Bearskin Lake 36
3. Awakening of a Vision 43
4. Missionary Wife 53
5. Service in the North 61
6. Lizzie Hears and Answers 71
7. Mary's Testimony 77
8. A Teacher in the Northland 81

PART TWO: CHRIST'S KINGDOM INCREASES

9. As Many As Received Him 95
10. Rejoicing in Heaven and in Red Lake 101
11. We Wrestle Not Against Flesh and Blood 107

12.	Go Home and Tell	116
13.	New Life for Lazarus	120
14.	Back to Bearskin	127
15.	Lessons from the Trapline	130
16.	Baptismal Trip to Fort Severn	135
17.	An Unexpected Camping Trip	141
18.	A Visit to the Bunkhouse	159
19.	Church Building at Bearskin	167
20.	A Servant Falls	171
21.	Incidents in the Air	177
22.	Expanding the Work	188
23.	Learning Proper Reserve	199
24.	Stuck in the Slush	204
25.	Finances	208
26.	Recollections of Service	211
27.	God Provides	218
	Epilogue	231
	About the Author	233
	Christian Aid Ministries	235
	The Way to God and Peace	237

NORTHWEST ONTARIO

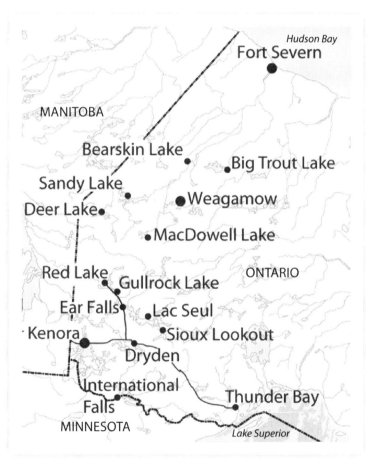

Contains information licensed under the Open Government License – Canada.

INTRODUCTION

God Gave the Increase is the result of Mission Interests Committee's (MIC) desire to document some of the early years of their work in Red Lake, Ontario, especially Ezra and Nannie Peachey's term there. The purpose of writing this book is to record historical facts about the work, but it is more than that. The committee desires to share with others some of the marvelous ways God worked in human vessels who answered God's call to this part of His vineyard. Instead of giving an exhaustive account of all who served there and in what capacity, this book is a compilation of inspiring accounts that MIC hopes will inspire others to joyfully dedicate their lives and talents to carry out the Lord's Great Commission.

The first part of this book tells the stories of various individuals who were involved in MIC's work in the North. In these chapters you will read of the Holy Spirit moving in people's hearts, calling them first to receive the Lord Jesus, burdening their hearts for the souls of men, and then motivating them to work for Him in northern Ontario. The second part of the book recounts a variety of experiences encountered by MIC workers during their service in the North.

These relatively few accounts represent the greater work of God as He deeply stirred the hearts of many Amish and Amish-Mennonite people in the 1950s and 1960s. When God moved these souls to deeper personal conviction and purpose, this resulted in a burning desire to help others find the abundant life in Christ Jesus.

MIC began as an entirely Amish entity. Its first mission venture was the opening of Hillcrest Home in Arkansas in 1953. At that time and throughout the initial meetings concerning the work in Canada, the members of the committee were all Amish and did not drive automobiles. Some of the Amish settlements represented by MIC, however, were already accepting the use of electricity and the telephone. Many of these groups later affiliated with Amish-Mennonites or Beachy Amish, and accepted the use of the automobile.

Throughout this book you will find references to Amish, Amish-Mennonites, and Mennonites. It is not the intent of MIC or the author to elevate one group above another. People from all these groups were involved in the work in Canada. Some workers went to the field as members of the Amish church and returned home as Amish. Other mission personnel who were members of less conservative churches worked harmoniously with their more conservative counterparts within MIC. Most of the native people

INTRODUCTION

of the North were not concerned with the different applications of Biblical principles and were content to refer to the various Anabaptist workers simply as Mennonites. This was most likely a consequence of Northern Light Gospel Mission's earlier efforts in planting churches.

※ ※

Some of the people you will read about in this book have already passed on to their eternal reward. Others are still living, some in the twilight years of their lives. I am grateful to all who so willingly provided the information from which these chapters were written. Much effort has been taken to portray people and incidents as accurately as possible. I thank all who supplied notes, reports, newsletters, and photographs to make this book possible. Many hours were spent on the telephone both interviewing and corroborating the information given. It is my desire that *God Gave the Increase* will not only be interesting, but also inspiring to you. At whatever stage of life you are, may you be thrilled to follow the Master wherever He may lead you. To God be the glory, great things He has done!

—*Robert Stauffer*

PROLOGUE

This prologue provides some of the historical background for the work of MIC in Canada. It tells of some of the open and closed doors faced by those who were attempting to answer God's call on their lives. Most of the information in this prologue was taken from a report compiled by Daniel Beachy, an early board member of MIC, who graciously permitted its use here.

※ ※

In 1955, a mission conference was held at Clinton Christian School near Goshen, Indiana. The conference lasted from Wednesday, August 17, until Friday evening, August 19. It was the sixth year in a row that this conference had been held. These conferences were sponsored by a group of believers who later became the Woodlawn Amish-Mennonite Church.

Over the three days of the conference, both lay members and ministers shared numerous topics that emphasized vision and missions. The Holy Spirit was moving people to a greater commitment to missions.

On Friday afternoon Harvey Graber had a topic, "Why Not Enter the Field?" suggesting the possibility of opening a boarding school for indigenous children in northwestern Ontario.

As a single man, Harvey had spent parts of several summers working with Northern Light Gospel Mission (NLGM) in Loman, Minnesota. NLGM's founder and leader, Irwin Schantz, was expanding that outreach northward to Red Lake, Ontario. Through him, Harvey learned firsthand of the need for someone to provide schooling for native children. No educational institution in Red Lake, governmental or otherwise, had opened its classroom doors to the indigenous children. Irwin was hoping someone would meet this need.

Harvey Graber's topic caught the attention of the assembled group, which included members of Mission Interests Committee. That year, the committee was comprised of Daniel Beachy and Harry Weirich from Indiana, Yost Miller from Ohio, Mahlon Wagler from Kansas, and Henry J. Yoder from Oklahoma.

At the conclusion of the Friday evening service, these men called a committee meeting to weigh the challenge Harvey had laid before them that afternoon. The committee invited former MIC participants with local and out-of-state ministers to join the meeting in an upstairs room. The meeting went past midnight, although not everyone stayed until it concluded.

A decision was reached in that meeting to consider starting a boarding school for indigenous children in northwestern Ontario,

Canada. Later in the summer, MIC asked three ministers who had been present at the conference to solicit direction from Irwin Schantz. These ministers were to seek and investigate possibilities for working in the area of northwestern Ontario where Schantz already had experience in working with the indigenous people.

The three ministers, Elam Hochstetler and Daniel S. Bontrager from Indiana, and Willie Wagler from Kansas, left by airplane and flew to Loman, Minnesota, on October 24, 1955. Irwin Schantz assisted them by flying them into Ontario. They would return on October 27.

The report that these men sent to MIC of their investigative trip indicated many opportunities among the native people for missions, but acquiring land for a school was not a simple matter, as it would have been in the States. The area in consideration was on a reservation for indigenous people, making real estate difficult to acquire. Also, the concept of a boarding school was not understood by those living on the reservation, and they questioned the need for it. Ontario law did not require children living on the reservation to attend school.

During the investigative trip, no clear understandings had emerged. There was confusion about international ownership of a property and working relationships on the ground. The information the men had received was vague. Although the possibility of mission work remained, there had been no definite developments; consequently, there was no feasible recommendation to offer. However, the trip members were not ready to suggest dismissing the endeavor.

Upon receiving their report, MIC continued to consider this

undertaking. They engaged in many telephone conversations among themselves and with their contacts in the Red Lake, Ontario, area.

The next MIC meeting was held at the Elam Hochstetler residence in Goshen, Indiana, on February 14 and 15, 1956. Henry Yoder from Oklahoma chaired the meeting. Committee members, along with other ministers, former MIC committee members, and other local interested persons were present for parts of the meeting.

Discussion about the possibility of a boarding school occupied much of the afternoon of the second day. It was helpful for the group to discuss the uncertainty that the October investigative trip had revealed. The three men who had taken the trip had little encouragement to give. At one point, the committee almost dismissed the idea of a school completely. The practical possibilities seemed too few.

Some of the younger persons present were more optimistic, and after prayer, the group made the decision to try again. Willie Wagler commented that perhaps they had been looking into the wrong end of the telescope! It was decided that Elam, Daniel, and Willie would make another investigative trip. They left Sunday evening, February 19, 1956.

On their second trip, the men still did not find an acceptable location, but they reached a clear enough understanding with the Red Lake officials that it seemed feasible to continue the pursuit. MIC continued to dialogue with Canadian officials about the undertaking.

At the same time, God was preparing couples who were willing to go to Canada and teach in the school. The venture was in motion again.

Correspondence with officials in Red Lake continued. Concrete planning began. Yost Miller, a builder from Millersburg, Ohio, drafted some building plans for a boarding school with dormitories upstairs and classrooms and living quarters on ground level.

On May 1, a group drove to Red Lake to check on possible locations and other details. The group consisted of two MIC committee members: Harry Weirich from Goshen, Indiana, and Mahlon Wagler from Kansas. They were joined by a former committee member, Ananias Beachy, from Kalona, Iowa, and two others, Moses Beachy from Goshen, Indiana, and Lloyd Gingerich from Plain City, Ohio. The group succeeded in finding a few possible locations for a school building. With the exception of Lloyd Gingerich, who stayed in Ontario to help Irwin Schantz, they all returned to the States on May 11.

Among the possible locations was a parcel of land on Skookum Bay with an empty gold miner's living quarters on-site. That building could be used to house a family. Another nearby building could be used for storage. The tract was large enough for a school building, and among all the possibilities so far, this seemed the most ideal.

While still in Ontario, the five brethren reported some of their findings back to MIC. Upon returning home, they presented a more comprehensive report. The possibility for a boarding school now seemed less feasible. They recommended that a regular elementary school for indigenous children be pursued instead of a boarding school.

MIC immediately attempted by telephone to rent the miner's house. They hoped to build a new two-room building, with a basement and indoor plumbing, on the premises, about five hundred feet from the miner's house. Their attempt was not completely successful, but renting the property still seemed possible.

Yost Miller and his family from Millersburg, Ohio, had committed to going to Red Lake for the summer of 1956 to lead the construction project with the help of volunteers. On May 6, 1956, Yost and Fanny Miller with their four children had come to Indiana with plans to continue to Red Lake, Ontario, for the building project.

The updated report from the MIC members who had traveled to the North was positive overall, but MIC still did not have complete clearance from the Canadian officials to begin the project. Yost called the contact person in Red Lake again to confirm the project before leaving Indiana but didn't make any headway. After several days, Yost began calling the officer in Ottawa, Ontario. Nothing seemed to be ready.

The Miller family continued their stay in the Goshen/Middlebury area, living in the basement of a friend's house. When time permitted, Yost worked part-time with Daniel Beachy and contractor David J. Miller.

After more phone calls to Ottawa produced no results, Yost made a trip by bus to Ottawa. He was able to get enough information and a clearer understanding of the necessary procedures for moving forward.

Later that month, Elam Hochstetler, Daniel Bontrager, Yost Miller, Dan Beachy, Harvey Graber, Harry Weirich, and Moses Beachy had a meeting at Harry's home to review and weigh the latest information from Yost and his Ottawa contact. Yost had discovered that many businesses rent existing properties and only a few own land themselves. Even the Red Lake Bank was on rented ground. Numerous residents in Red Lake were actually squatters, not landowners. Yost had discovered that the property MIC wanted to purchase did not have a clear title, and he was uncertain how to proceed.

In light of these things, it was decided to wait longer for satisfactory clearance from Ottawa. It also became clear that it might be easier to acquire land in the Red Lake area after living there for a period of time.

Finally, after four weeks in Indiana, Yost received enough satisfactory information by telephone to feel comfortable to go north. He and his family left by train on June 4, arriving in Loman, Minnesota, on June 6. Irwin Schantz accompanied them across the border.

TIME LINE OF MAJOR EVENTS IN MIC'S WORK IN THE NORTH

1955–1956	MIC develops a burden and vision for a school for indigenous children in Red Lake, Ontario. First buildings are completed and school opens in fall of 1956.
1956–1963	Red Lake Indian School is in operation in Red Lake, Ontario.
1963–1964	The church at Red Lake Indian School experiences revival and rapid growth.
1964	Periodic Bible schools are held at school facilities for approximately eight years.
	Mission outreach expands to Lac Seul and Hudson with the David Herschberger family.
1966–1968	The David Mosquito and Elijah Stoney families move back to Bearskin Lake.

1968	Ezra Peachey begins flying a small airplane in order to minister on reserves when requested.
1971	Mission outreach expands to Sioux Lookout with the Wayne Schrock family.
1975–1988	Red Lake Christian School operating under Believers' Fellowship.[1]
1981	Mission outreach expands to Sioux Narrows with the Lorne Kuepfer family.
1988	Mission outreach expands to Kenora with the Melvin Stoltzfus family.

MIC Field Directors

1956–1960	Harvey Graber
1960–1986	Ezra Peachey
1986–1998	Wayne Schrock
1998–present	Darrell Nisly

---

[1] The work MIC started in Red Lake with the Indian school and church was officially incorporated in 1972 as Believers' Fellowship. This name became commonly used to identify the work in Hudson, Sioux Lookout, Sioux Narrows, and Kenora. In Red Lake, though, the "Indian School" term stuck for many years, since that is how it was first identified.

PART ONE

THE WORK BEGINS

1
IN THE BEGINNING

Yost and Fannie Miller and family

"Well, we are another step closer to Red Lake," Yost Miller said to his wife as he settled back in the bus seat. "Are you comfortable?"

"I will be fine," Fannie replied quietly as she cradled two-year-old Ellis in her arms. "These bus seats are more confining than the seats on the train. I hope our little boy can get a good nap."

"I'm relieved the border crossing went so smoothly," Yost added. "I got the feeling our family was something of a novelty to those officers."

"It appeared that we were somewhat unusual," Fannie agreed. "We sure got a lot of stares. I wonder how many Amish families have entered Canada through this entry point."

"Oh, I would guess some Amish have come across to fish," Yost ventured, "but the immigration officer acted as though it was something out of the ordinary to have a whole family come for several months."

Turning in his seat, Yost observed that Clarence, six, and Esther, four, were asleep. He caught the eye of his eight-year-old son, Nelson, sitting across the aisle. "What do you think of Canada?" he asked.

"The trees are so different," Nelson answered. "In Ohio most trees have large limbs. Here, the trunks are straight like telephone poles, and the limbs are very thin. I wonder what the difference is."

Yost nodded his head. "Perhaps it's because the growing season is much shorter up here and the weather gets bitterly cold."

The Miller family had left their home in Millersburg, Ohio, in early May of 1956 and traveled to Indiana. They had committed to spending their summer leading out in the construction of the school that was planned for Red Lake, Ontario. In Indiana, Daniel and Viola Beachy had shared their home with the Millers as together they tried to get clearance for the project from the Canadian officials. In spite of many phone calls, nothing seemed to be certain enough to proceed. As they waited, Yost had worked part-time in carpentry until they were reasonably sure they would be able to build the school. Then Yost and his family had traveled by train from Indiana to International Falls, Minnesota. There they had purchased bus tickets to Kenora, Ontario, where they would stay overnight. Another bus ride would transport them to Red Lake. They were not sure what would await them at the end of their travels.

"Welcome to Red Lake," Irwin Schantz said to the Millers as they pulled into the settlement at last. "The house where we live is called the Howey House. We are happy to have you stay with us. Our accommodations are nothing fancy, but we welcome you to share what we have. We have been praying for Mission Interests Committee in their plans to start a school for native children. Until now, these children have had no opportunity here in Red Lake to get even a basic education. For some reason, the provincial authorities have little interest in opening the public schools to them. I believe there are parents here who will welcome the opening of a school for their children."

The next day Yost constructed beds so that his family wouldn't have to sleep on the floor. Then he began investigating the property where MIC hoped to construct the school.

"It appears it may be next week before it works in other people's schedules to check out the site," he reported to Irwin on Friday morning. "In the meantime, is there something I might be able to do for you?"

Irwin thought for a minute. "Yes, there is," he said presently. "We have purchased property to build a house for our family. It is along the road that winds north out of town toward Forestry Point, where the government has a fire-fighting base. Would you be willing to start digging the footer for our house if you have spare time? As much as we would like to get started, though, I don't want to take you away from the purpose for which you came."

Yost began the hard work of digging dirt to prepare to pour the footer for Irwin's house. That Friday night he wrote in his little diary, "Mosquitoes and flies are real bad."

Prior to coming to Red Lake, Yost and the MIC leaders had frequently contacted authorities in Red Lake and in Ottawa about acquiring land. Making progress from a distance had been slow at best. Now, living in Red Lake and working face to face with the land agent, Yost was soon able to work things out. By early July Yost had a letter in hand describing terms for leasing a property on Skookum Bay that included an abandoned miner's house.

A local insurance agent, Jack Dunn, was interested in MIC's efforts to open a school. Jack was instrumental in working out some details, and by Monday, July 9, Yost was ready to proceed. He went to the bank in Red Lake and got a $2,100 loan to purchase the house located on the leased property. The Yost Miller family and Lloyd Gingerich then moved into the miner's house. In the following days, Yost prepared a revised building plan for the school.

Lloyd, from Plain City, Ohio, had come to Red Lake several months earlier intending to help build the school facilities. When those plans were delayed, he worked alongside Irwin Schantz. The months were not wasted. He and a Northern Light Gospel Mission (NLGM) staff person, Sadie Yoder, befriended local indigenous children, and on May 20 they started a Sunday school for those children. When the weather was nice, Sunday school classes were held on a large, flat area of bedrock across the bay from NLGM headquarters. Throughout the summer, more and more children attended this time of singing and Bible stories. Workers who came later to help build the school got involved in this Sunday school outreach during their time in Red Lake. By fall, about two dozen children were coming to Sunday school regularly. Through wise use of their spare time, Lloyd and Sadie did much to convey the mission's goodwill and love for the native people.

After moving into the miner's house, Yost and Lloyd needed to get the property surveyed. To do that, they cleared paths through the forest for the surveyors to get proper sightings.

Once the boundaries of the property were established and the site for the school determined, the real work began. Lloyd and Yost began clearing trees from the building site on August 14.

∧ The Red Lake Indian School was located west of the town of Red Lake, close to the Forestry Service. It was at the lake's edge, allowing the Indians to come from all directions with their canoes.

Yost ended up driving into town quite often to arrange for an excavator, cement mixer, and the delivery of building materials. On August 18, a lumberyard owner, Earl Smith, brought his equipment and dug the basement. On August 21, Yost wrote in his diary, "Started building forms for basement walls."

One day Yost and Jack Dunn went to Manitou Falls to look

at some barracks that were available free of charge to anyone who would tear them down. The buildings had been erected for workers when a hydroelectric dam was being constructed in the area. Volunteers spent many hours salvaging lumber from the barracks to use in the school's first buildings.

"Would you drive me over to Gustafson's sawmill?" Yost asked a worker one morning. "We need to purchase more lumber to frame the school, and I have a list here of what I need."

Yost was in for a pleasant surprise when he met the big Swede who owned the sawmill. "Good morning, Mr. Gustafson," Yost greeted him. "Do you still have some lumber for sale?"

"Reckon I got a few sticks left," the friendly man replied, a big smile on his face. "What will you be a-needin'?"

Yost went over the lengthy list of lumber that was still needed for joists, rafters, studs, and sheeting. "I guess this is more than a few sticks," he said, smiling.

"I think ve can help you out," replied the lumberman, "and I'll tell ya someting else. I hears ya gonna have school for dem Indian kids. I reckon it's a shame that the regular school here won't be havin' 'em. I likes what yous are doing and I wants to help my little bit. Tells you what, those one hundred twenty 2 x 4 x 10s are on me. Reckon I's can help that much."

"Why, thank you," Yost replied. "I didn't expect you to give us anything for free. God bless you for your generosity."

Many work crews came from the States. Men with last names

like Glick, Lapp, Stoltzfus, Shetler, Yoder, Troyer, Miller, and many more made the trip to Red Lake to work for a week or two. The accommodations were nothing fancy. A secluded spot on the shore of Red Lake provided the bathing facilities. The men wanted to work, and the project proceeded smoothly.

One day Irwin Schantz's son, Chris, drove Yost 268 kilometers down to Vermillion Bay and then west on the Trans-Canada Highway to Kenora. They came home loaded with plumbing and heating supplies. God provided workers with the skills needed to do the plumbing and heating installation.

One night Yost and Fannie had a long conversation before they drifted off to sleep.

"The building is coming together quite rapidly," Fannie said, speaking softly to avoid waking the children. "I didn't know you knew how to do so many things."

"I know that God has had His hand in all of this," Yost acknowledged. "Sometimes I wonder what my mother would say if she saw what was happening here."

"Why do you say that?"

"When I was still a teenager, my heart was not in farming. Daddy was already gone, and Mother was trying to guide our family the best she knew how. One day I told her about my desire to learn carpentry instead of pursuing farming. I know that really concerned Mother."

"How did you know that?"

"She told me. Mother said if I did not farm, I would never amount to anything. In her mind, carpentry was outside what we as a people were known for doing."

"Was that discouraging for you?" Fannie asked.

"Somewhat," Yost answered. "While I knew she meant well, I just couldn't seem to get excited about farming all my life. I tried farming for ten years, but I couldn't seem to make a go of it. During those years, I got books on engineering and learned how to properly construct a building. I studied a lot. Some people thought I was wasting my time. But God had given me that interest, and I decided to apply myself to learn what I could about the building trade."

"It blesses me," Fannie interjected, "to see you leading these groups of men week after week. I feel so proud, no, that isn't the right word, grateful, yes, grateful to be your wife. I am so happy to be here with you this summer in this project."

"I am happy, too, that you and the family are here! And there's something else that's special to me this summer. Remember how I've told you about working in the Civilian Public Service camps before we were married?"

Fannie nodded.

"That is where I really became acquainted with Mennonites and learned what they believe. The way they understood the Bible and lived out those principles in everyday life had a tremendously positive influence on me. That is when I became aware that my life and my body belong to the Lord. I am bought with a price. God wants us to glorify Him with our bodies and our lives. After all these years, it is such a joy again to be working together with Mennonites who have come to help build the school."

Silence reigned for a few moments as Yost reflected on years gone by.

"Something else comes to mind . . . I don't know whether I ever told you about it."

"What's that?" Fannie wanted to know.

"During my teenage years when I knew I didn't want to farm, I also got excited about body building."

"Body building?" Fannie was surprised.

"Yes, I signed up for a Charles Atlas body-building course. It was one of those self-help things advertised back then to help a person develop a muscular body. I am ashamed now to have gotten involved in something that was so attractive to the flesh. My time in CPS with those Mennonite men led me to understand that my life is not about bringing attention and glory to myself, but to the Lord. Realizing that, I renounced my involvement in things like body building. Now there is a deep satisfaction and gratefulness in my heart for the Lord's leading in my life. It feels so right to be here, using our time and energy to further His kingdom."

"Thank you, dear, for sharing those things with me. Truly, God moves in mysterious ways, His wonders to perform."

"Thank you for listening," Yost added. "You are God's precious gift to me, and I thank Him for you and the four children He has given us. But now I'm thinking I should get some sleep. Goodnight, sweetheart."

The work on the school building progressed rapidly. Some workers who had come earlier in the summer returned later to help more. They came from many states, stretching from Pennsylvania to Oklahoma.

One happening of that summer is forever etched in the minds of the Miller family. One warm day when they and their visitors

^ The walls of the Red Lake Indian School building go up.

were hard at work, one of the men looked up. "Look, there is little Ellis coming, and his clothes look wet," he said, pointing to the little boy coming from the direction of the lake.

Work stopped as Yost hurried to his son. "Whatever happened?" he said quietly to no one in particular.

Yost's oldest son Nelson ran to meet Ellis too. "Daddy, he's completely soaked," Nelson exclaimed.

Yost comforted his young son, then picked him up and started following his trail of drips toward the lake. His wonder increased as the wet footprints led him onto the dock and down the sloping surface into the deep water at the end of the dock. He stood there in amazement. Somehow his little boy had fallen off the dock into the water. That explained why Ellis was wet from head to foot.

But how did he manage to make those wet tracks coming up the sloping dock from the deeper water?

The family and others gathered around, trying to make sense of what they saw. It seemed impossible that the two-year-old would have been able to get out of the deep water and walk up the sloping dock as the tracks indicated he had. Finally, after weighing all the possibilities they could think of, only one remained. God had sent an angel to rescue Ellis from drowning!

Yost removed his hat and bowed his head. Simple words of gratitude came from his lips as he thanked the Lord for His protection and deliverance that day.

God had used Harvey Graber to spur interest in the Red Lake school one year earlier at the sixth Annual Amish Mission Conference. As plans for the school in Red Lake began to materialize, MIC recruited Harvey to be the principal and head teacher at the new school.

As soon as Yost notified the Grabers of the purchase of the miner's house, Harvey and his wife Miriam began preparing for the move. They had two children, and Miriam was expecting another child. Mission Interests Committee purchased an old, yellow, one-ton, step-van truck, afterward affectionately referred to as the "bread truck." With their personal belongings and a large supply of groceries and canned food for the mission packed inside, the Grabers left Indiana and headed to Red Lake on September 11. Several other men accompanied them to work on the building project.

^ The Harvey Graber family.

The group only got as far as Gary, Indiana, when the truck gave them mechanical trouble. They made several phone calls and were able to get the problem fixed. They had more vehicle trouble in Eau Claire, Wisconsin, and were delayed about a day until the truck was fixed.

It took almost a whole day to cross the border into Canada because of their special circumstances. They required proper immigration clearance since they were being sent by a church to teach in the new school. Finally, toward evening, the group was cleared to head north.

Just a few miles north of the railroad town of Red Lake Road, they encountered a steep hill. In 1956 the road was not yet paved. The truck got stuck in gravel part way up that hill. Harvey backed down and tried again, being a little more aggressive with the throttle. The truck got stuck again. Harvey backed up again, this time until they were on the top of the next small rise to the south. Now it was all or nothing. He accelerated through all three gears and kept the throttle wide open. Were they going to make it?

When they were close to the top of the hill and the truck had lost most of its speed, several of the men jumped out and pushed for all they were worth. They kept the bread truck moving slowly until it crested the hill. Praise the Lord; they had made it! The truck finally pulled into Red Lake on Sunday, September 16. The school property became a buzz of activity as the team made the final push to open the school.

By September 23, the school building was far enough along that Sunday school could be held there for the first time. Some local youths and a few adults attended.

˄ The Grabers' home during their first year in the North.

On October 2, the Yost Miller family bid farewell to their friends at Red Lake. Irwin Schantz flew them to Baudette, Minnesota, in NLGM's new Cessna 180.

By October 23, the school building was ready for the first day of school. Twenty students were enrolled. For the first two semesters, Lloyd Gingerich taught the younger children, and Harvey Graber taught the older students.

The school for indigenous children had become a reality. God's prompting and the obedience of dozens of volunteers made it possible. God would use the ministry of the Red Lake Indian School to bring more disciples into His kingdom.

God used Yost and Fannie Miller's working vacation that summer of 1956 to accomplish more than just the building of the school. A compelling interest and vision for the work of the

∧ Rough shell of the Indian School building.

mission was born in their eight-year-old son, Nelson. He returned as a sixteen-year-old to supervise the building of a sanctuary onto the school, which was used to accommodate the large number of people coming for church services. Later Nelson and his wife Sarah served a term as staff in Red Lake. Nelson also led out with MIC building projects in Hudson and Sioux Lookout in later years.

∧ Grades 1 and 2 at the Indian School.

2
EXODUS FROM BEARSKIN LAKE

Elijah and Emma Stoney and family

"Emma, I've got to do something," Elijah Stoney informed his wife. "There is so little I can do to earn a living here in Bearskin Lake. We are always low on money, and groceries are so expensive. I don't like to keep charging at the store. Sometime our credit limit will be reached."

Emma lifted her eyes from the moccasins she was beading and gazed at her husband. He was wiry and strong and not afraid of hard work. Even though they seldom discussed it, she had known for some time he was feeling badly about their financial situation. It was not their custom to blurt out feelings quickly. Inwardly she was glad he had spoken what was heavy on his heart. "What do you think we should do?" she asked.

"When I lived in Winnipeg before we got married," he said, "there was plenty of work. But that is so far from here. I wonder whether I might find work in Sandy Lake. That is a lot closer."

"But how would you get to Sandy Lake?" she wondered.

"Well, I have the boat and could travel by water," Elijah replied. "That wouldn't cost as much as chartering an airplane."

Elijah paused, and Emma could see he was thinking about such a trip. Emma knew that before float planes had been introduced in the North, travel on the river systems had been common. Some of her ancestors had made a yearly trek downstream from Sandy Lake all the way past Bearskin Lake to Fort Severn on the Hudson Bay. She remembered her grandmother telling about her husband. Emma's grandfather would leave his family early in the spring, soon after the ice had left the lake and before the leaves had come out. By the time the long journey was completed, months later, the trees had already shed their leaves. Going downstream with light loads to carry over the portages took a fraction of the time required to go back upstream. Coming home, their packs were heavy and they had to paddle against the swift current. When they came to rapids, everything had to be unloaded and carried across the portages. Then the men would load the packs again and paddle on. Sometimes they were able to leave the supplies in the canoe and use a rope to pull the vessel upstream through the rapids. It had been dangerous work but had saved a lot of backbreaking carrying. Emma wondered whether her husband even now was considering the danger and the hard work such a trip would require. True, Bearskin was between Sandy Lake and Fort Severn, but the journey her husband was proposing was all upstream. Then Elijah looked up.

"Do you have a better idea?" Elijah asked.

Emma shook her head. "No, can't say I do."

Several days later Emma and her children stood on the shoreline and watched Elijah and his boat become smaller and smaller in the distance. "How long will it be till I see him again?" she asked herself.

* * *

Elijah was weary when he came into the east end of the sprawling Sandy Lake. He had endured days of rain, wind, mosquitoes, and black flies. Bannock[1] and black tea, liberally laced with sugar, had provided the energy to go on. The river had yielded plenty of walleye to eat when he took the time to catch them. But he sure was looking forward to eating and sleeping in a cabin without the pesky mosquitoes biting him all the time! *And yes, hopefully a job will be available*, he thought.

Unfortunately, no work was available for Elijah in Sandy Lake. There were numerous reports of job openings in Red Lake, though. The gold mine was hiring. Sawmills needed workers. In the growing economy of Red Lake, other employment might also be found. Elijah began investigating how he could get to Red Lake. He ended up selling the boat he had brought from Bearskin and using the money to buy airfare to Red Lake.

In Red Lake, Elijah found employment at McDougall's sawmill. With steady work, his financial situation began to improve. He wanted his wife to be with him. That fall Elijah heard of a plane that was going to Bearskin Lake, and he made plans for

---

[1] Bannock is a type of fried bread, commonly eaten by the indigenous people.

his wife and daughter, Elsie, to fly out on the backhaul. He sent instructions for her to leave their belongings behind and come out with the pilot.

Elijah came to meet the float plane as it taxied toward the dock in Red Lake. Would Emma and Elsie be on board? The pilot turned off the motor and carefully guided the drifting plane beside the dock. Elijah could see his wife inside waiting to get out. He stepped from the dock to the plane float and took Emma's one hand as she grasped the plane's fuselage with her other. She felt around with her foot until she located the step fastened on a float strut. Another step and she was down on the float with her husband. Elsie was more nimble, and soon all three were together on the dock.

"*Boozhoo,*"[2] Elijah said. "It is sure good to see you both again."

"*Boozhoo*, Elijah," Emma shyly answered. "I'm glad to be here with you."

Before long, all three were sitting in Elijah's little house, drinking tea. "Did you have a smooth flight?" Elijah wanted to know.

"It wasn't too bad when we left Bearskin," Emma answered. "But the closer we got to Red Lake, the rougher it became. I think it bothered me more than Elsie. It is sure good to be on solid land. I'm happy we are together again, but I sure wish our older children could be here too."

"I agree," Elijah replied. "The Mennonites have started a school for native children here at Red Lake. The Mennonites seem like good people and really care about us. Before they came, there was

[2] *Hello.*

∧ Staff photo taken in front of the "bread truck" school bus during the summer of 1958.
   L to R: Mose and Ada Beachy with two sons, Myron and John; Amy Byler, Marietta Hochstetler (now Mrs. Jonathan Stoltzfus), Arie Miller (now Mrs. Daniel Hochstetler), Noah Hochstetler and wife Loretta, Miriam and Harvey Graber with three sons, Millard, John Howard, and Merlin; Ollie Troyer, Moses Mast.

no school here for native children. But that has changed, and now our children could live with us here and also go to the school."

"It was hard saying goodbye to them when they left for the Pelican Residential School in September," Emma replied. "It would be so nice to have them come here. We could be together as a family, and they could get the schooling they need."

The next day Elijah went to see Harvey Graber, principal of Red Lake Indian School. Harvey's wife, Miriam, answered Elijah's knock.

"*Boozhoo,* Elijah," she greeted him. "*Biindigen.*[3] Harvey is in the other room grading some papers. He will be happy to see you."

"*Boozhoo,*" Harvey smiled as he got up from his chair. "Good to see you again, Elijah. I heard your wife came in on a backhaul."

"Yes, that is right," Elijah answered. "It is good to be together with her again."

A few minutes of silence prevailed, and Harvey waited patiently for Elijah to say what he had on his mind.

"Would you like some tea?" Harvey asked.

"*Miigwech,*[4] that would be nice," Elijah replied.

"You are welcome," Harvey said.

After a few minutes of sipping tea, Elijah lowered his cup and raised his gaze to Harvey's face. "Emma and I have been thinking about our older children and their education," he began. "Right now they are at Pelican Residential School down near Sioux Lookout because there was no school for them in Bearskin. We were wondering whether you would have room for them here in your school."

"Yes, we would be happy to have them," Harvey replied. "When are you thinking they would start?"

"We will have to work that out with the school at Pelican. But it is likely they will be sent here at Christmas break since both Emma and I are now living in Red Lake. Could they begin when classes start after Christmas?" Elijah inquired.

"Yes, that would be fine," Harvey assured him. "I look forward

---

[3] *Come in.* Pronounced BEEN dĭ gĕn.

[4] *Thank you.* Pronounced MEE gwĕch.

to meeting them and having them in school. I am sure you will be glad to have your family together again."

3
AWAKENING OF A VISION

Ezra Peachey

The story of the Red Lake Indian School is woven closely to the story of a young man from Belleville, Pennsylvania. The Lord had a calling for Ezra Peachey, but first He chose to lay a burden on his heart and then prepare him for service. The burden that ultimately took Ezra to the North began far away in a hospital in Mexico.

❦ ❦ ❦ ❦ ❦ ❦ ❦ ❦ ❦ ❦ ❦ ❦ ❦ ❦ ❦ ❦ ❦ ❦ ❦ ❦

They had gotten far more adventure than they had bargained for. Now, as the faint hints of early dawn gradually pushed aside the blackness of night, Ezra stirred in bed. Jumbled thoughts began crowding his mind as consciousness returned. Where was he? How had he gotten to this place? Labored breathing from across the makeshift room informed him he was not alone. A muffled groan came from another direction. What was going on here? Oh yes, that's right—an accident last evening. Slowly Ezra started sorting out his thoughts, trying to make sense of what had happened.

He recalled his restlessness that autumn on the family farm in Belleville, Pennsylvania. His father had died thirteen years earlier, and the burden of the farm work had fallen largely on his sons' shoulders. One by one, Ezra's four older brothers had married. Ezra's mother was a good manager and organized the farm work well for Ezra and the two brothers and three sisters younger than he. But that winter, at twenty-two years of age, adventure had beckoned to Ezra. Sylvanus and Simon thought they could handle the farm work, and Ezra was free to go.

Ezra and two of his friends, Alvin Yoder and Crist Kurtz, briefly considered exploring Florida. But even then, in 1948, they perceived that Florida was getting too crowded and full of tourists. Having read in *The Budget* of an Amish settlement near Mission, Texas, they set their sights on that small city, just a few miles from the Rio Grande River.

In Texas they had met two conservative Mennonite bachelors from Vineland, Ontario, who were traveling to a colony south of Mexico City for a visit. One of them had a car and invited Ezra and his friends to travel with them. When they got to the border crossing into Mexico, they discovered that although American citizens did not need passports to enter the country, Canadians did. One of the Mennonite men from Ontario did not have a passport, so he was denied entry. The other one, Levi Houser, the owner of the car, had his passport, so he along with Ezra, Alvin, and Crist had been able to continue driving south.

The first fair-sized city they had come to was Reynosa. They had inquired about staying at a motel. When their request for lodging had been accepted, a gate was thrown open and they drove into an enclosed yard where the car would be secure overnight. After supper, a restful sleep, and breakfast, they had resumed their journey southward.

On the afternoon of their second day in Mexico, the men had arrived at a town that had motel accommodations. There they had needed to make a decision. Should they stay or push on to the next city? The weather was nice and the sun was still fairly high in the sky, so the men had decided to go farther.

It had been dark as they approached the outskirts of San Luis Potosi. A truck had been coming toward them with its headlights on high beam.

Ezra twisted in his bed. His memories had awakened him fully. He could visualize clearly the bright lights of the approaching vehicle. He remembered their car veering off the road and plunging down an embankment. He relived the horrifying saga of their headlights illuminating a man leading a donkey and the sickening thud as their car ran over the animal. Killing the donkey was terrifying, but the car had still kept moving rapidly. It had careened on, plunging down over a five-foot retaining wall on the edge of a lower road. The heavy car had bounced and skidded across the road until it had plowed into a house, knocking a hole in the building itself.

Levi had been tightly pinned behind the steering wheel, causing the horn to blow continuously. Alvin had been launched from the backseat through the windshield and was semi-conscious and moaning. The owner of the donkey had been hurt, but his injuries were not life-threatening. All five had been taken to a medical clinic attached to a large Catholic church. The room was approximately sixteen feet wide and thirty feet long, with a curtain blocking off the far end. One bed sat against the left wall; Ezra was assigned to this bed. Three other beds were on the opposite wall, and Ezra's companions slept there. The owner of the donkey was given a mat on the floor.

Ezra remembered that nurses had come in to give Alvin a shot to relieve his pain. His other two companions politely and steadfastly said, "No shot." The nurses were persistent, but they were met by equally settled sentiments not in favor of the shot. Ezra realized then that the nurses may try to give him an injection as well, so he quickly pretended to go to sleep. He did not want a shot, nor did he want to reject their offer. His ruse apparently worked, because when the nurses came to his bed, they found him already "asleep." They apparently assumed he didn't need the pain reliever, so they left without touching him.

Now, as the room brightened in the early morning light, Ezra's senses picked up some activity behind the curtain at the end of the room. Rolling over in bed, he stretched his neck out to peer beyond the edge of the curtain. On the other side was a chapel replete with images of Mary, Jesus, and saints from the Bible. Ezra had read of such things but had never seen them in person. It was particularly gripping to him to see people coming before those images that morning, bowing down, praying to them, and kissing their feet. *These people need the Gospel*, he thought.

As Ezra recounted those moments sixty-four years later, his eyes got misty and he was solemn. "I was never quite the same after that," he said in a choked whisper.

The day after the accident, an officer from the British Consulate came to the clinic. The consul helped the men settle up for the damages they caused. The young men paid the owner of the donkey twenty dollars to cover the cost of his animal.

"I need to take one of you with me into Guadalajara," the consul said. "I will have to file a report there about what happened in the accident. Which one of you will go?"

Ezra was chosen to accompany the man to the big city. The officer provided a hotel room for him that night. In the morning he returned and took Ezra to the insurance office. There Ezra gave a report of the accident. When he was finished, the lady at the desk spoke to the British consul. "Should I call the police?" she asked.

"No, don't call; just let it go," the consul replied.

"Why did she wonder about the police?" Ezra asked the consul when they had left the insurance office.

"If I had agreed to let her make that call," he replied, "you would be headed for jail."

"You mean they would put me in jail even when I was not the driver?" Ezra asked incredulously.

"Yes, they would. Sometimes that is the way they do things here," he replied.

Ezra stayed in Guadalajara for several days until Crist Kurtz and Alvin Yoder rejoined him. While Ezra wanted to go on to their original destination, the other two men had seen enough. They wanted to return to the States. Levi stayed for nearly a month until his car was fixed so that he could drive it home.

The three men left Guadalajara and got a ride into Mexico City.

There they purchased bus tickets to return to Mission, Texas, where they found jobs with Texas Gold, a grapefruit juice processing company. The men were employed there for two months. They canned the juice, labeled and boxed the cans, and stacked the boxes in railroad cars.

Next, Ezra went north to Kalona, Iowa, to visit two men who had previously worked in Harrisburg, Pennsylvania, on a farm for mentally disabled men. During their time in Harrisburg, those two men would sometimes drive up to Belleville on their weekends off.

Ezra's visit with them in Iowa fanned the flames in his heart to get involved in mission work somewhere. Thoughts of volunteer service were in the forefront of his mind as he returned to his family in Belleville.

Later, Ezra wrote to the Mennonite Central Committee inquiring if they were doing any work in Mexico that he could become involved with. MCC had nothing for him in Mexico, but they suggested he go to Puerto Rico instead. So Ezra went and spent a year and a half working on a research farm with goats—lots of goats. He communicated frequently with his mother by mail. Some of his correspondence follows:

> *Dear Mother,*
>
> *I am enjoying my work here in Puerto Rico. As I wrote before, we have a lot of goats to care for on this research facility. There are many poor Puerto Ricans living nearby who need milk but don't have the money to buy it. But if they are willing to take care of a goat, they can have the*

milk. I am glad we can help people in this way.

How are you doing back home? I miss you all but I believe this is where the Lord wants me for now. Please write when you can. I enjoy your letters.

Ezra

Dear Mother,

I have something to ask you about. I remember talking to Father after he was ordained. He told me of his brother-in-law who had gone to high school and then later was ordained as a minister and bishop. Father told me his relative felt that schooling was a good influence on him and helped in some way to prepare him for his work as a minister.

I have been thinking much about God's call on my life. I have not forgotten the scene I saw in that clinic in Mexico. God has laid a burden on my heart for the souls of men, and I often wonder how I should prepare myself to be useful to the Lord. Many nights I have lain awake thinking about this. Lately it seems God is speaking to me about going to school to get some training. If I recall correctly, I think Father would approve of this were he yet living. What do you think?

Sincerely, Ezra

Dear Ezra,

I appreciate hearing from you whenever you can write. I am grateful God is using you there in Puerto Rico and that you enjoy what you are doing. You wrote about your thoughts of going to school. That is somewhat of an unsettling thought to me right now. Perhaps it might be wise for you to come home for a while. What do you think?

Love, Mother

Several letters later . . .

Dear Ezra,

I have been thinking much about what you wrote a while back concerning going to school. I have been praying about it as well. If you still believe God would have you go to school, then you go ahead and follow the Lord. I give my consent. God bless you, my son.

Love, Mother

Ezra returned from Puerto Rico determined to pursue further

education. He was also interested in finding a life partner but decided it would be better to remain single until his schooling was finished. Ezra began his studies at Eastern Mennonite College (EMC) in Harrisonburg, Virginia, at age twenty-four. He went to EMC for four years and then studied an additional two years at Eastern Mennonite Seminary. He graduated at age thirty. He was not as successful in waiting that long to pursue a wife. During his fourth year at EMC, Ezra started dating Nannie Peachey. He was upfront with her about God's calling upon his life. Even though God had not revealed the details of where he was to go and when, Ezra wanted his prospective life partner to know what she would likely be facing. Ezra and Nannie were married between the fifth and sixth years of his schooling.

Following graduation, the Peacheys returned to Belleville, and Ezra taught in the Belleville Mennonite School. This was somewhat a community school with Amish, Mennonite, and Amish-Mennonite children attending. Ezra taught Bible in both junior high and senior high classrooms. In addition he taught biology, history, and Problems of Democracy.

During the two years that Ezra was teaching at Belleville, he and Nannie were listening for further direction from the Lord. For a while they considered a request to work with Amish-Mennonite Aid (AMA). AMA was beginning a work with refugees in Berlin, Germany. But two things did not give Ezra and Nannie peace about that request. First, they were expecting a child. Secondly, Ezra would have had to break his teaching commitment part way through the school year. He did not believe it was right for him to do that.

Howard Hammer was an evangelist who had held meetings in Belleville before Ezra and Nannie were married. It was under his ministry that Nannie, already engaged to Ezra, had responded to an invitation indicating a willingness to go into God's vineyard for service. Howard was envisioning a work in Brazil among the indigenous people there, and he invited the Peacheys to join him. Yet Ezra and Nannie did not have peace in their hearts about pursuing that either.

Their call to Red Lake, Ontario, came in the form of a letter from Mission Interests Committee. The year was 1957. MIC requested that Ezra and Nannie come to Red Lake and lead out in summer Bible school. Two years later, they were formally invited to move to Red Lake, and Ezra began teaching at the Red Lake Indian School. God had awakened a vision in their hearts, prepared them for service, and then called them into the arena where their life's work would take place.

4
MISSIONARY WIFE

Nannie Peachey

Nannie was twenty-one years old when she and Ezra were married on August 25, 1955. Some time before this, at a hymn sing, this soft-spoken man had asked for the privilege of taking her home. It had come as a surprise to Nannie, because Ezra was nine years older than she was. Nannie had never considered that he might ask her.

Nannie could not confide in her mother, since she had passed away several years earlier. But Nannie and her father had a good relationship, and both of them respected Ezra for his character and interest in missions.

"He was older, and I perceived he was a spiritual man," Nannie said, remembering her early impressions of Ezra. "Knowing he was interested in mission work was not a worry to me at all. My father also had a heart for mission work in northern Michigan and helped there whenever he was able. Seeing my dad's fervor for the souls of men was instrumental in shaping my attitudes toward these things. I knew when Ezra asked me that I might end up as a missionary's wife, but my family and I were at peace with that. During our courtship, Ezra often talked of the burden on his heart for the souls of men. Six months after our relationship began, he asked some pointed questions about my willingness to spend my life in such endeavors. Later, when Ezra raised the prospect of marriage, I was ready to follow him wherever God might lead."

Ezra and Nannie did not take a wedding trip simply because, as Ezra said, "I didn't have that much money." He had invested the funds he had at Eastern Mennonite College, preparing for his life's work.

When the Peacheys traveled to Red Lake in the summer of 1957 for two weeks of summer Bible school, Nannie's father, Jonathan, and her sister, Martha, accompanied them to help and observe this new work. It was Nannie's first exposure to missions in a cross-cultural setting. She and Ezra left their first baby, nearly a year old, with Nannie's sister in Pennsylvania.

Between forty and fifty children came to the school building for several hours of teaching each day. It was a full but rewarding two-week period for both students and staff. Nannie was one of the teachers, and she was delighted and grateful to God that her students seemed to enjoy the experience. The staff had fun angling for walleye and northern pike when time permitted. The fish fry that followed was delightful! During their two weeks in Red Lake, Ezra and Nannie got to know many of the native people. This was their first mission endeavor as a couple, and they had much to reflect upon as they made the long drive back to Pennsylvania.

By the summer of 1959, Ezra and Nannie had been asked by MIC to move to Red Lake and take up a teaching position at Red Lake Indian School. They packed their belongings and arrived in Red Lake at the beginning of July.

One of the highest desires of a godly wife is to be a suitable

^ Ezra and Nannie in the 1960s.

helper for her husband. Nannie was no exception. Between nurturing their children and tending to the household tasks of washing, cooking, and mending, Nannie's days were full. Many evenings were spent visiting in the homes of their neighbors.

Sundays were days of ministry. One of Nannie's Sunday school students was Jim Keesic. Many years later, Jim would look back on those early years with fond memories. "Nannie was my Sunday school teacher," he recalled. "One of the songs I remember was,

'Saviour, teach me day by day, love's sweet lesson to obey.' We used to sing that song often."

In addition to regular mid-week church services, other short informal meetings were held in various homes. Along with others, Ezra and Nannie would visit two or three homes in one evening. They would sing a few songs, and Ezra would share a short meditation. Sometimes he would ask one of the young men to share something as well. Following prayer and farewells, the group would be off to another house. If nobody was home, they went to the next place. This was the pattern for many years.

One of the challenges Nannie faced was the language barrier. Many of the older women she worked with knew little English. Nannie knew that if she wanted to communicate with them, she would have to learn to speak their language. She really worked at

∧ Nannie visits with friends at MacDowell Lake.

it. Of course, she made grammatical errors. Rarely would someone point out her mistake. It was often a bit of shy, muffled laughter that alerted her. It was not the laughter of mockery, however, but an amused appreciation that Nannie was trying so hard. When that happened, Nannie was humble enough to ask what she had said wrong and how to say it correctly. After church services or when visiting in homes, Nannie would keep practicing her new tongue. Agnes Keesic, a native woman, spoke of how much she appreciated Nannie's effort to learn and speak their language. Her mistakes didn't really matter. "She speaks Indian," was a succinct and sincere compliment to this missionary wife.

Having visitors was usually refreshing and encouraging. It was always a time of extra work, as well. Sometimes Ezra and Nannie knew when guests were coming. At other times, visitors showed up unexpectedly. Expected or not, visitors needed to be fed, and it was often Nannie's responsibility to cook for them.

One day a carload of visitors arrived late in the morning. Nannie was instantly calculating in her mind the possibilities she had for lunch. As she silently pondered the inventory of supplies available, she remembered, *That's right, we have a pretty nice batch of fish on hand. Yes, I'll fry fish for lunch.*

The fillets of fish were taken from the refrigerator. While the frying pans were heating up on the stove, Nannie busied herself coating the fish in a mixture of cornmeal flour and seasonings. Some butter was added to the frying pans, and before long a pleasant sizzling sound was heard. Delightful aromas wafted from the kitchen.

"Something smells really good," one of the visitors remarked.

"You are making my mouth water."

Nannie smiled and nodded her head. She remembered the delight of her first taste of fried walleye, and she wanted their visitors to enjoy it as well.

When she had a plateful of fish prepared, Nannie announced that lunch was ready. Everyone gathered at the table, grace was said, and everyone dug in. Everyone that is, except Nannie.

She kept on frying fish. Many of the guests were on their second or third helping when one of them noticed that Nannie was still busy in the kitchen and hadn't even taken time to eat.

"Nannie, have you had any fish to eat yet?" one of them asked. The answer was obvious.

Soon after those visitors left that afternoon, another group showed up, and once again Nannie cooked for them, providing their supper. She did it without complaining. Many years later she would reflect on those times. "I don't know how I did all that," she recollected. "I am not able to do that anymore."

In spite of the extra work, it was a real encouragement to Ezra and Nannie to have visitors. Many traveled great distances to see the work they had read or heard about. Many offered words and prayers of encouragement. Many of the visitors came to see the work they had been supporting financially. Some of the visitors became burdened with a desire to return home and live more simply and sacrificially after they saw first-hand what God was doing in Red Lake.

One year Nannie had a sewing class where she taught neighbor ladies how to make blankets. Since most of them had no means of transportation, Nannie would drive a VW bus around to their homes

^ Nannie and her Indian friends enjoy making comforters.

to pick up the women. On one particular day, a local lady, Elizabeth Rae, was sitting up front with Nannie. As their van came around a curve, a vehicle coming from the opposite direction crossed the center of the road and hit them hard. Nannie was not seriously hurt, but both of Elizabeth's legs were broken. She was taken to Winnipeg for surgery and was there a long time recuperating. After that, she was somewhat crippled and always had to wear a brace.

"She never held it against me," Nannie said. "We often went out to Winnipeg to visit her. She never seemed to be against us because I was driving when the accident happened. She was a Christian and had attended church for a long time. We remained friends for the rest of her life. Her husband later came to profess peace with God as well."

Greta Mosquito was a special friend to Nannie. They learned

to know each other in the early years of the Peacheys' work at Red Lake. Greta and her husband, David, received Jesus Christ into their lives during these years. When David and Greta's family moved back to their home to Bearskin Lake, it was difficult to stay in touch. In the following years Nannie would occasionally accompany Ezra on a flight into Bearskin to visit the Mosquito family. The advent of telephone service to the northern reserves provided a way for more frequent communication. When Nannie was asked about the basis of her friendship with Greta, she answered, "We both had a good relationship with the Lord." Their intimate walk with God provided context for much womanly sharing between them as wives, mothers, and spiritual pilgrims in the kingdom of God.

5
SERVICE IN THE NORTH

Susie Bontrager

What a way to plunge into teaching for the first time! Susie Bontrager was twenty-three years old and facing her first teaching assignment at the Clinton Christian School in Indiana. The year was 1957, and sitting before her were twenty-six first graders. She did not have a helper, at least not one with flesh and bones. The second year her load was only slightly lighter, with twenty-four students.

MIC held mission meetings nearby during the winter of 1958–1959. Prior to those meetings, the Lord had been preparing Susie for her future work. She had no idea what God had in mind, but she rightly sensed in her spirit that the Lord had a special work that would be revealed to her in His time.

During the meetings, the MIC board met privately with Susie and asked her to consider teaching at the Red Lake Indian School. Susie immediately knew in her heart this was what God had been preparing her to do. In early 1959, she agreed to go to Red Lake to teach. She moved to Ontario late that summer.

"The road leading up to Red Lake was very poor," Susie recalled many years later. "There was a lot of construction going on, and we thought it took a long time to cover the 105 miles between Vermillion Bay and Red Lake."

When Susie first arrived, she taught the three lower grades in the Indian School. "When I began," Susie remembers, "many of the youngest students first needed to learn the English language. Most of my second and third graders already knew some English and were better able to do their lessons.

"I really enjoyed my students. Each year had its own challenges. When spring came in Red Lake, there was usually an influx of native men and their families from northern communities. They came seeking work, and their children wanted to come to school. It was not easy to determine what grade level each child was ready for, but we managed somehow. It could be challenging to find enough school desks for the new arrivals."

Most of the students enjoyed recess, even during the winters when the mercury plunged low in the thermometer. When it was bitterly cold, Susie planned indoor activities for recess since they had no gymnasium at the school. However, when it warmed up to at least ten degrees below zero, the class would bundle up warmly and go outside to enjoy a game of tag for ten or fifteen minutes.

The bitterly cold weather factored into the death of a teenager who lived about a mile past the school. It was a sad time for the girl's family, the Keesics, and for the school staff who had come to know the young girl. No one knew just where the girl had been and what she had been doing one cold night, but her frozen, lifeless body was discovered near her house the next morning. She had been unable to make it home.

Because so much was unknown about the circumstances of the teenager's death, the authorities took her body to Dryden, Ontario, to perform an autopsy to determine the cause of death. When the autopsy was complete, Ezra and Nannie volunteered to assist the Keesic family by bringing the body back to Red Lake for the funeral and burial.

It was a bitterly cold evening when the Peacheys arrived in Dryden and loaded the girl's casket into their VW van for the 133-mile trip back to Red Lake. Before they had reached Vermilion Bay, twenty-eight miles west of Dryden, the van broke down.

"What will we do now?" Nannie asked her husband.

Ezra thought through some possibilities for a few minutes and made up his mind. "First, I need to get to a telephone and call home. I'm hoping Mahlon Nisly can bring the bread truck down and take us and the casket home. He's familiar with the quirks of driving that vehicle since he drives it to haul students to school and church."

"Will he come that whole distance alone in this cold?" Nannie wondered.

"Oh, I'm sure he could drive here by himself," Ezra replied, "but maybe one of the other staff could come along and keep him company. I'll recommend he bring Susie along. She was a good friend of this girl, and I believe Susie will give up her sleep to assist in this way."

Sure enough, Mahlon and Susie braved the cold and lonely highway to bring Ezra, Nannie, and the deceased girl home to Red Lake that night.

Death touched another local family during Susie's Red Lake years. Johnny and Mary Perrault and their two boys, Jimmy and Danny, lived within walking distance of the school. Susie soon learned to love this family. Two months after she arrived in Red Lake, the Perraults had a daughter, and they named her Susie.

Sometime later, another baby, a boy, was born into the family. From birth, he was quite sickly.

^ Johnny and Mary Perrault with son Danny at Red Lake Indian School.

Early one morning Susie jerked to attention. "Who is knocking on the schoolhouse door?" she asked her roommate, Lizzie. "The way they are knocking, it must be something urgent."

Susie finished dressing and hurried from their upstairs apartment down to the school entrance. When she opened the door,

Johnny and Mary Perrault were standing there with a deep sadness written across their faces. Mary was holding a tiny, lifeless body lovingly in her arms. Johnny managed to speak. "Our baby died during the night. Would you be willing to prepare him for burial? We have brought some other clothes along to dress him."

Tears welled up in Susie's eyes as she reached out her arms to receive the little one. In those fleeting moments she remembered many happy times of visiting in the Perrault home. In this moment, their grief became her grief. Tears flowed unashamedly down her cheeks as she took the little bundle.

"Oh, I am so sorry," she wept. "I am glad to help you in this time of sadness." Lovingly she washed the tiny body that was only a few days old. Together, she and Mary clothed the tiny form and gently laid it in the tiny casket Johnny had brought along.

"Thank you," Johnny and Mary said to Susie.

"You are welcome. I am glad to be able to help," Susie answered.

At the funeral service that followed later, the school staff gathered around to support the Perrault family in their grief. One song in particular became etched in Susie's memory. She would reflect upon the words of that song for years afterward.

> Safe in the arms of Jesus,
> Safe on His gentle breast;
> There by His love o'ershaded,
> Sweetly my soul shall rest.
> Hark! 'tis the voice of angels
> Borne in a song to me,
> Over the fields of glory,

> Over the jasper sea.
> Safe in the arms of Jesus,
> Safe from corroding care,
> Safe from the world's temptations;
> Sin cannot harm me there.
> Free from the blight of sorrow,
> Free from my doubts and fears;
> Only a few more trials,
> Only a few more tears.[1]

Susie enjoyed visitors. Her sister Anna made the trip to Red Lake a number of times, once in the dead of winter.

"Would you like to go snowshoeing this afternoon?" Susie asked Anna late one Saturday morning while she was visiting. "It's a beautiful, sunny day, and it's not too cold for an outing. What do you say?"

"That sounds like a lot of fun," replied Anna. "Where will we get the snowshoes?"

"I talked to Mahlon last evening after he took the school children home," Susie told her. "He knows where he can borrow several pairs."

"Who all is going?" Anna wanted to know.

"Mahlon, Lizzie, you, and me," Susie answered. "I think you will like the challenge. Maybe I should warn you, though. You

---

[1] Text by Fannie Crosby, 1868. Public domain.

might trip with the snowshoes and fall down. But don't worry; it happens to everyone who learns to snowshoe."

After lunch, the four strapped on the snowshoes and headed out. It was one thing to walk on the packed trails and roadways and master the purposeful steps. It was quite another thing to head into virgin snow. The snow was deep and fluffy.

Before long Susie heard a gasp and a muffled scream. Turning, she saw Anna lying on her back in the soft, powdery snow and flailing her arms as she tried to get up.

"Let me help you, sis," Susie said as she carefully circled to where Anna lay. She helped Anna get to her feet and dusted some of the whiteness off her clothes. "It makes you feel pretty helpless, doesn't it?"

"I'll say," admitted Anna. "There is nothing to get a hold of when you're upside down in that fluff. Thanks for helping me up. Let's have another go at it."

A few minutes later Anna was in the snow again. Susie couldn't help laughing.

"I wish I had a camera," she exclaimed.

"I'm glad you don't," shot back Anna. "I'm not sure what I did wrong this time. All of a sudden I couldn't keep my balance and it was like, 'here we go again.'"

Mahlon stood nearby as Anna stood up. He offered a bit of advice to Anna. "I learned that you have to make deliberate steps. Make sure the shoe you are stepping with is clearing the snowshoe buried in the snow. Otherwise, when you take the next step and try to pick up the buried foot, it gets caught under the other shoe. That puts you off-balance, and from that point there is nowhere to go but down."

"I think that is what happened this time," Anna laughed. "I'll see if I can get this act together yet."

The four spent a pleasant afternoon together, and by four o'clock they were nearly back at the school. They stopped for a breather.

"I believe the temperature is falling rapidly," Lizzie exclaimed. "I got pretty warm earlier, but now I feel the chill keenly."

"Yes," Mahlon agreed. "Take a look at the western sky. I enjoy looking at it on these cold winter evenings. See how the yellow and gold colors change into pink and purple and then to dark blue? God sure uses a tremendous variety of colors to paint the sky. I also like seeing the long shadows cast by these pines in the lowering sun. In fact, it almost looks as if they are pointing the way home."

"You describe it so well, Mahlon," Susie agreed. "Right now I think I will follow those shadows back to the school. I'm getting a bit chilly myself. Besides, I think we need to warm up my sister with some hot chocolate."

✦ ✦

Susie experienced some health challenges in Red Lake. She had gotten a medical exam in preparation for entering Canada to teach. Her iron had been very low, and the doctor in Indiana had given her some iron shots. The fall of 1959, her first in Red Lake, Susie was sick for five weeks with boils under her arms. The boils were so bad that they kept her awake at night. When the boils finally cleared up, she got pneumonia and struggled with it well into December. Nonetheless, Susie kept teaching through both of these illnesses. During Christmas break, she finally regained her health. Sometime later when she visited her doctor in Indiana, Susie discovered that other patients who received the same iron shots had also gotten boils and pneumonia.

In May of 1962, Susie contracted another illness. Within a few days she was so weak that one afternoon at school, she dismissed the children to go outdoors and play. She sat on the steps and watched them until it was time for them to go home. When she went to the doctor in Red Lake, she was diagnosed with infectious hepatitis, or hepatitis A, as it is called today. Susie was quarantined in the back room above the school for several weeks. Lizzie Yoder finished out the school year for her. It was a discouraging time for Susie, and as summer advanced, her health was slow in returning.

"Brother Ezra, I need to tell you something," Susie said one summer evening. "I'm not getting my strength back very quickly at all. If I don't get better soon, I don't think I will be well enough to teach in the fall."

"What are you thinking, Susie?" Ezra wanted to know. "Do you think we should look for another teacher?"

"That's why I wanted to talk to you," Susie replied. "I would feel better if you could arrange for a replacement for me."

Ezra tried to find a teacher, but they were not able to find one by the time school started in September. Susie's sister, Anna, came up to help for the first month of school. Susie taught in the morning and then rested. Anna took care of the children over lunch and then had the children's story time and rest period. That was a big help to Susie. It took about ten years for her to fully recover from her bout of hepatitis.

Susie taught four years at the Red Lake Indian School, until it was closed in 1963. It was with sadness that she left the North and the people she had grown to love. However, some of her friendships with these people continued for many years after her return to the States.

But relationships with the people of the North was not the only thing that came out of her years of service there. God used those years to bring Mahlon and Susie together. Their relationship progressed from being co-laborers in the North to being united in a godly marriage.

6
LIZZIE HEARS AND ANSWERS

Lizzie Yoder

"How did your Sunday school class go today?" Susie Bontrager asked her roommate one Sunday.

"Oh, it went all right," replied Lizzie. "Our lesson was on Jesus feeding the five thousand. The children seemed interested enough in the story, but I wonder sometimes why they don't answer questions more readily. Do the students speak up in your school classes during the week?"

"Not as much as I would like," Susie answered. "But I have learned that the native people are more comfortable with silence than I am. So don't take it too personally if they don't talk a lot. Can you tell if they are paying attention?"

"Most of them do," Lizzie said, "but especially Josephine. Even though she hardly utters a word, I can see in her eyes that she is getting the message, even when others around her are misbehaving. Peter is a precious little boy, but he is always squirming and seems to delight in pestering those next to him."

"Yes, he is a little troublemaker," Susie agreed. "It seems to me he is trying to get attention. One of the challenges I face in teaching is learning not to play his game— you know, not rewarding his misbehavior by giving him the attention he is trying to get. I guess most teachers face these things sooner or later."

"That's an interesting thought. There is so much I have yet to learn about teaching!" Lizzie exclaimed. "It doesn't seem very long ago that I came here to teach summer Bible school. Up to that point, I had no teaching experience."

"How did you happen to come to Red Lake?" Susie wanted to know. "I don't think I ever asked you that."

"It is sort of a long story," Lizzie ventured.

"I have plenty of time," Susie told her, "so tell me about it."

"Well," began Lizzie, "I was in voluntary service at Hillcrest Home in Arkansas caring for the elderly. I had been serving for some time, and I knew there was a waiting list of applicants wanting to volunteer there. Working at the home was a real blessing, but God impressed on me that I should terminate to give others a chance to serve."

"So what did you do?" Susie wanted to know.

"I told the administrator at Hillcrest what I believed God was asking of me," Lizzie explained, "and he graciously accepted my decision to move on. Before I left, I received a telephone call from my doctor's wife back in Ohio, asking me to consider working for them again. I had worked for them before serving at Hillcrest, so I agreed to her request, but I told her I wanted to work only until June. So when June arrived, the big question in my mind was what God had for me next.

"I was living in a duplex in Ohio with my parents at the time," Lizzie continued. "Across the road was a large woodlot. Late one evening I walked over there to be alone with God and try to discern His will for me. I still remember sitting on a log praying and pleading, 'Lord, what do you want me to do?' Shortly after I prayed, I heard a horn blow. The sound came from the direction of our house so I figured somebody might be signaling for me to come. Sure enough, it was Anna Bontrager, my friend from Indiana. She stopped in to tell me that she and a few others would be leaving for Red Lake, Canada, around the end of June to teach Bible school. She invited me to join them. Because it was right at the time my job with the doctor would be concluding, I took that as the Lord's prompting to go.

"But," Lizzie went on, "I told Anna that I had no teaching experience and would be a real novice. Anna assured me there would be something for me to contribute and urged me to accept the invitation. I agreed to go, believing this was the Lord's next step for me."

"So that is how you came to Red Lake!" exclaimed Susie. "How did the teaching go?"

"It was a wonderful chapter in my life," answered Lizzie. "I had a delightful little class of third graders. Teaching was a stretching experience, but I had the assurance that God wanted me there. When Bible school was over, I returned to Ohio."

"So," Susie probed, "how did you end up coming back as the cook?"

"Well, Sadie Swartzentruber was cook when I first came to teach Bible school, and Moses Mast was also serving here. They began dating and eventually got married. After their marriage, God led them elsewhere. That's when I got a call from Harvey Graber asking whether I'd be willing to come and take Sadie's place as cook at the school. I sensed this was the Lord's leading and was ready to come back."

"Thanks for sharing your story with me," said Susie. "It's encouraging to hear how the Lord leads people where He wants them to go. I'm so glad he brought you here, Lizzie. I appreciate your friendship, and I'm so glad for someone to talk with after my day in the classroom. You're a good listener."

"I feel the same way about you, Susie. Thanks for being my friend," Lizzie replied.

"Do you ever get tired of cooking lunch for forty students?" Susie wondered. "It must take a lot of planning and work to keep the staff and students fed each school day."

"Yes, it was an adjustment for me. But I enjoy the challenge," Lizzie reflected. "It sure is different than cooking back home though."

Susie commented, "When I am eating pears or applesauce, I often wonder who the kind people were who worked to home-can all this food. I suppose we may never know. Our supporters must have spent many hours preparing these foods to lighten our load here on the mission field."

"That is certain," responded Lizzie. "And I wonder who the people were that supplied that semi-load of Spork[1] to Northern Light Gospel Mission. It must have cost a bundle of money to buy

---

[1] A canned meat product similar to Spam.

that amount. Irwin Schantz was so kind to share a big portion of that canned meat with us. All that Spork makes one economical way for us to provide a good meal each day."

"Yes," Susie agreed. "And just how many ways have you learned to prepare Spork? I am amazed at the various ways you use it. Right off the bat, I can think of Spork and beans, fried Spork sandwiches, and of course Spork by itself as meat. I like the line in Spork's advertisement: 'Cold or hot, Spork hits the spot.' "

Lizzie smiled and added, "I've also ground it up and used it to make meatloaf. Most of the students and staff seem to enjoy that very much. Also, have you noticed how much the children like spaghetti? I've sometimes substituted ground Spork for beef in that dish."

Susie laughed. "Last week when you mixed moose meat and Spork together in a casserole, did you hear what the table conversation was about? Someone called the mixture Spook and oh, did we have fun with that."

Lizzie changed the subject. "If I'm to be in a good humor tomorrow morning, I should get to bed. Monday mornings are always so busy."

"Sounds like a good idea," admitted Susie. "Guess I'll do the same."

❄ ❄ ❄ ❄ ❄ ❄ ❄ ❄ ❄ ❄ ❄ ❄ ❄ ❄ ❄ ❄ ❄ ❄ ❄

In addition to cooking, one of Lizzie's jobs was supervising the school girls for their weekly shower and hair washing. Many of their homes did not have running water, and the opportunity to bathe at school was a real blessing. Lizzie also enjoyed teaching the older girls to sew. Her goal was for each girl to make a blouse for herself.

Quite often, evenings were spent visiting the homes of students and those who attended Sunday services. One evening a group of staff, including Ezra, Nannie, Susie, and Lizzie, decided to call on a family in Balmertown, seven miles to the northeast. They had an enjoyable visit and soon it was time to leave for home.

"Thank you for allowing us to come and visit," Nannie said.

"Please come and see us sometime," invited Susie. "I really enjoyed this time with you."

"Yes," chimed in Lizzie. "When you come to Red Lake, please drop in. That would be special."

All the staff walked out to their vehicle while Lizzie lingered behind to talk a minute or so longer. When she joined her fellow workers, she was puzzled as to why they were laughing. It almost seemed they were laughing at her.

"Hey, what's so funny?" Lizzie demanded.

"You told those folks that when they come to Red Lake, they should drop in," some of the staff chuckled.

"And what's so funny about that?" Lizzie began, until suddenly it dawned on her. "No, I wasn't inviting them to jump in the lake," she chuckled.

7
MARY'S TESTIMONY

Mary Mast

Christians everywhere will identify with the conviction of being called to serve the Lord, sometimes in far-off places. Some will identify with the call to be senders, to work hard and live simply in order to financially support those serving elsewhere. Mary Mast's testimony not only shows what God did in her heart; it also reveals the unique way God led her to be about her Father's business. Here is her story:

"I grew up in an Amish family in Indiana and didn't know the Lord. In the summer of 1954, a friend invited me to go along to work at a children's home in Kentucky. When the summer ended and my friend needed to return to teach school, I stayed to help in the dormitory and kitchen.

"At the children's home, many of the staff often spoke about being 'saved.' A single mom who had repented of her sin and responded to God's message of salvation worked there. She enthusiastically related to me how she had found the Lord and was thrilled to be His disciple. Several of the staff kept after me about the need for Jesus Christ in my heart. Someone asked me whether I know that I am saved. I didn't even know what that meant.

"A question formed in my mind, and I finally was able to put it into words: *Do I have to do something bad before I can get saved?* It was an honest question. The answer was revealed to me in God's Word from Romans 6. 'Shall we continue in sin that grace may abound? God forbid!'

"God was convicting me of being a sinner and was drawing me to Himself. One night at a Pilgrim Holiness meeting I responded to an invitation to receive Christ. That changed my life. I became hungry to read the Bible, and reading God's Word opened my eyes to truths I had never known. Knowing I was His child filled my heart with a deep peace and joy.

"I was so grateful to the Lord for saving me that I began seeking how I might be useful in His kingdom. The Lord impressed upon me the idea of getting nurse's training as an avenue of service. I graduated as a Licensed Practical Nurse in 1958. God provided Christian fellowship for me. I worshipped with a small group near Clinton, Indiana. Harvey and Miriam Graber, who attended there as well, had become involved with the Red Lake Indian School in Ontario. Harvey asked me to come teach Bible school one summer. That was the beginning of my involvement with the work at the school and later with NLGM.

"While I was in Red Lake, God made it possible for me to use my nurse's training as a means of supporting the work of MIC's

MARY'S TESTIMONY

˄ Mary Mast with her summer Bible class.

school. I was hired as a nurse at the Red Cross Hospital and lived with the MIC staff. My wages were turned over to the mission, and I received the regular support of a single staff: fifteen dollars per month, housing, and food. That was plenty for me. My financial needs were small. In addition to employment at the hospital, I regularly taught Sunday school and also helped with cooking as my schedule permitted.

"Working with the Grabers, Peacheys, and single staff was such a highlight in my life. Lizzie Yoder and Susie Bontrager were especially close spiritual friends to me. I thrived in a setting where people loved the Lord and were seeking to win souls for Him. What a joy to be able to speak freely about spiritual things and rejoice with each other as we recognized God's hand in our life experiences.

"The greatest thrill of my life is to belong to the Lord. He has led me along in both good and difficult circumstances. At 79 years of age, I have never lost the wonder of it all."[1]

---

[1] After working in the hospital in Red Lake, Mary Mast served as a public health nurse at Poplar Hill, Grassy Narrows, and Deer Lake. She and Christian P. Stoltzfus were married in 1978.

8
A TEACHER IN THE NORTHLAND

Paul and Martha Miller

FIRST IMPRESSIONS

"Paul, would it suit you and Martha to come to our place for some refreshments after we close up here?" Ezra asked one Sunday evening after church.

"Thank you. I don't think we have anything planned, but let me check with my wife, and I'll get back to you," Paul replied.

Twenty minutes later Paul Miller, his wife Martha, and their young daughter were sitting in Ezra's house enjoying a snack.

"What did you think of your first Sunday evening service in Red Lake?" Ezra asked Paul.

Paul took a few seconds to collect his thoughts. "I have three distinct impressions. The first has to do with how many people were crowded into the school basement. It was really encouraging to me to see such spiritual interest in these people. Is this normal?"

"Yes," Ezra answered, "that is typical of the last few years. God has definitely moved in many hearts, and we are grateful for the adults and children who have professed Jesus to be their Lord."

"The next thing I noticed has to do with the man who preached the message this evening," Paul continued. "Who is he again? I've forgotten his name."

"His name is Jimmy Mezzatay, from Cat Lake," Ezra explained. "He came to faith in Jesus Christ without a lot of direct contact from other Christians. Most of what he learned came from reading the Bible. I like to use native speakers when it is feasible because they speak the language. How did you like listening to a message through an interpreter?"

"I was able to follow along well enough. Why is it though, that it seems to take the interpreter longer to say in English what was said in the indigenous language?" Paul wanted to know.

"I think if you heard someone interpreting the other direction," Ezra answered, "from English into the local language, you would probably notice the same thing. It often takes longer to say something because the interpreter may not be able to convey a word from one language to a single word in the other language."

"That makes sense," agreed Paul. "The third impression was that Jimmy seldom looked out over the audience. Instead, he kept his gaze lowered most of the time while he preached. Is that typical?"

"Yes, Paul, that is typical of many native speakers. It is one of many cultural differences we find in a setting like this. As you get acquainted with the work here and speak up front on occasion, you will find that the audience is more comfortable if you do not look directly at them. It is one of the things we needed to learn," Ezra admitted.

A GLIMPSE INTO PAUL'S DAY

"Breakfast is ready," Martha said quietly to Paul, not wanting to awaken Hilda. They bowed their heads together in prayer, thanking God for His many blessings. Paul asked God to protect Martha as she cared for Hilda and the child they were expecting. He also prayed for wisdom in his teaching that day.

After prayer, Martha lifted the lid off the small kettle on the table, and a fragrant cloud of steam dissipated into the air.

"What is this?" Paul asked. "I don't recognize it."

"It's Red River Cereal," Martha answered. "Nannie told me about it the other day. It's something they have learned to enjoy. I thought maybe we should give it a try."

"Smells good enough to me," Paul replied. "How do we eat it?"

"The Peacheys put a little brown sugar on it for sweetening and then add some milk, just like we do for oatmeal. The label says it is made of wheat, rye, and flax."

As they finished eating, Martha asked, "What do you think about this cereal?"

"It's not bad at all," Paul answered. "I think I could learn to enjoy it. How about you? Do you like it?"

Her reply was interrupted by the sounds and vibrations of the garage door being opened below their apartment. Paul glanced at his watch as the motor in the old yellow bread truck started. By now benches had been installed in the truck, and it was used to transport students back and forth from school as well as to bring people to church services.

"Well, Mahlon is leaving right on schedule to pick up the students," Paul said as he rose from the table. "I had better be getting

^ The bread truck provided school and church transportation.

over to the classroom myself. There are a few things that need my attention before my little scholars arrive."

He pulled on his winter coat and hat and reached for the stack of graded papers. "Will you and Hilda be joining me for lunch at the school today?" he asked.

"Yes, we will," Martha replied. "I really enjoy that contact with the students. See you then."

Paul descended the stairs to ground level and briskly walked the short distance to the school building. Susie Bontrager was already in her room, preparing for the students in the first two grades. Paul taught grades three through six. Together, Susie and Paul taught about two dozen students.

Paul had grown up in Kansas and, as a student, had been well acquainted with multiple grades in one classroom. Now that he was on the other side of the desk, he better appreciated the skill required to keep several classes running smoothly. Typically, while the other grades were occupied with lessons at their desks, one grade would be called up front to take their places around a table.

^ The VW bus was primarily used to transport people to school and church services, but it also met other transportation needs. Here Mahlon Nisly and students are pictured with the bus.

Paul would review the work the students had done at their seats and then give them instructions for the next lesson.

Paul quickly learned that not all students are adept at learning. Some picked up new skills and information easily while others had to put a lot of effort into learning. It was both a joy and a challenge

∧ Paul and Martha Miller with daughter Hilda arrived in 1961.

to work with his students as they developed academically.

Following the afternoon classes, while Mahlon drove the students home in the bread truck, Paul spent an hour or so grading papers and preparing his lesson plans for the next morning. Then it would be time to return home to his family.

As he would open their apartment door, he would hear the patter of Hilda's tiny feet as she came running to meet him. "Daddy," she would say excitedly as he would stoop to give her a big hug. It wasn't long until Paul would be seated, reading a book to his daughter.

MAINTAINING ORDER
"Hello, Paul, come on in." Ezra invited Paul Miller into his office. He noted the serious expression on Paul's face and closed the door.

"What can I do for you?"

"Maggie[1] is being difficult today," Paul began. "She is not applying herself to her work and will not cooperate in class."

"Have you tried to probe deeper to find out why she is acting like this?" Ezra wanted to know.

"Yes," Paul replied, "but when I ask her a question, she just glares at me with a sullen expression and then tries to ignore me. Her behavior is having a negative influence on the rest of the class."

"How would you like me to help?" Ezra asked.

"Would you be willing to talk with her?" Paul requested. "Somehow, I have not yet established myself with her as a person who will be obeyed. Maybe she will listen if you talk to her."

"I will come and talk with her at recess," Ezra promised. "Would you keep her back when the other children are dismissed to play outside?"

"Yes, I will do that," Paul replied. "Thank you so much."

Ezra met with Maggie during recess. He found her as sullen and uncooperative as Paul had described. In his gentle and firm manner he informed her, "Maggie, you are going home." His eyes communicated the seriousness of her bad behavior, and from his tone of voice Maggie knew there would be no negotiating his decision. She was taken home for the rest of the day. From that time on, Paul had good cooperation from Maggie.

SEIZING OPPORTUNITIES

One of the ways Paul blessed others during his time in Red Lake was by donating blood when the Red Cross put on a blood drive.

---

[1] Pseudonym used.

Paul did so regularly, and one day after he had given a pint of blood, he met Johnny Perrault, who lived a short distance down the road from the school.

"*Boozhoo,* Johnny," Paul greeted him.

"*Boozhoo,*" Johnny returned.

Paul knew little of the native tongue and was glad that Johnny understood English quite well. Paul felt an inner prompting to speak of the blood drive with him.

"The Red Cross is having a blood drive today. Are you planning to donate blood?"

Johnny looked up briefly; then he slowly shook his head. "Oh, I don't suppose they would want my blood."

"I do think they would want your blood, Johnny," Paul replied. "The Bible says God made all nations of men of one blood. I'm sure the Red Cross does not accept or reject blood based on skin color."

After a bit more casual conversation, Paul and Johnny each went their own way. That evening at the supper table, Paul shared the incident with his wife. "I don't know what Johnny did with that thought," he told Martha, "but it was a moment God gave me to speak for Him."

UNCERTAINTY

During the 1962–1963 school year, Ezra began talking of phasing out Red Lake Indian School. The school had been started seven years earlier to provide a basic education for native children. At that time, those children were in a kind of no-man's land between federal and provincial jurisdictions. Now the situation had changed. Red Lake had opened its public schools to indigenous students, and Ezra pondered long whether they should continue the school and add junior high, or close the school and focus the mission's resources more directly on spiritual aspects of kingdom work. Already, some of their former students were studying in the public schools. In the summer of 1963, the Red Lake Indian School was closed.

Les Fawcett, the District Superintendent of Indian Affairs, was acquainted with the Red Lake Indian School. When he heard it was to be shut down, he came to inquire whether Paul would be willing to come to Sioux Lookout. Les wanted Paul to serve as a liaison for Pelican Residential School students who were being integrated into the public school system in Sioux Lookout. The job included administering standardized tests to discern the proper grade placement for these students. Paul accepted Mr. Fawcett's offer of employment.

Paul faced some opposition in Sioux Lookout. The Anglican clergyman who was in charge of the school did not like that Paul wore his plain suit. The Anglican headmaster was concerned that Paul may be trying to introduce a church teaching program to the school.

Even though the Millers were no longer under his mission leadership, Ezra felt a sense of responsibility to support Paul and Martha in the troubles they were facing in Paul's new job. In October of that year, the Peacheys traveled to Sioux Lookout to visit them. When Paul explained the nature of their difficulties, Ezra encouraged him not to fight, but to wait and see what would happen. He supported Paul in his desire to not compromise his beliefs to fit in with the secular expectations. Paul and Martha were very grateful for Ezra and Nannie's concern and the advice they gave them.

In the end, Les Fawcett wearied of the clergyman's complaining and offered Paul a teaching position at Round Lake. The teacher at Round Lake had just been moved to Sachigo Lake to fill a more urgent need there. Paul accepted that offer. He taught two years at Round Lake until Northern Light Gospel Mission invited him to come to Poplar Hill Development School. Paul served as teacher and principal there for ten years.

REFLECTIONS AND CROSSES
If Paul had been able to order the events of his life, he would have chosen to be a dairy farmer. But God had something else in mind for him. Between Paul's first and second birthdays, he became afflicted with a hip condition known as Legg-Perthes disease. The ball of his hip joint never developed properly, which resulted in weakness and eventual lameness in that leg.

This disability was both a cross and a directive for Paul. There were many physical things he was not able to do, and God used that to steer his ambitions toward things he could do. During his late teenage years, he began to focus on learning to teach. He saw teaching as both a means to support himself and an avenue through which he might serve the Lord. In reflecting on his path through life, Paul acknowledges God's hand in ordaining or permitting his trying circumstances.

Some people like warm weather. Others enjoy the cold and the challenges that go along with living in sub-zero conditions. Paul's sentiments were very much in line with the former, not the latter, but God had called him to the North. Those who knew Paul well seldom heard him complain about the cold. Later he admitted, "The winters seemed terribly long. In our fourteen years in the North, I never got to the place where I could say I enjoyed the cold. Four times I experienced 58 degrees below zero Fahrenheit, and once minus 60. But because the cold was inextricably linked to the work to which God had called us, I tried to have a positive attitude toward the cold."

When spring finally came the first year that Paul was in the North, the melting of the accumulated snow pack made many little streams of water, all rushing to the lake. The warmth of the sun was excuse enough to remain outdoors a bit longer than usual. The babbling noises of rushing rivulets was so enjoyable to Paul that he took a cassette recorder and captured the tinkling and splashing noises generated by the melted snow. He welcomed the return of warmer weather.

HEART SECRETS

Many conservative Anabaptist men who have been ordained to public ministry have had some intuition of this calling much earlier in their lives. In most cases these feelings were kept close to the heart and revealed only to trusted confidants who would not misuse such information.

By the time Paul was courting Martha, he had already sensed God's call to some form of preaching ministry. Early in their relationship, Paul knew it was appropriate to share this calling with Martha for her consideration.

Years later, when life led them to Poplar Hill Development School, Paul regularly brought a Sunday morning message for staff and students at the school. Various times, in the privacy of his own thoughts, he wondered, *Is this what my sense of calling was about?*

After returning from the mission field in 1975, Paul soon found himself among eight other brethren nominated for a double ordination to the ministry in their local church. Paul's subsequent ordination was a precious affirmation of the call he had sensed from God and for many years secretly pondered in the privacy of his heart.

PART TWO

CHRIST'S KINGDOM INCREASES

9
AS MANY AS RECEIVED HIM

The church services held at Red Lake Indian School were well attended. Many were hungry for the Word of God and came regularly to hear it proclaimed. Numerous attendees seemed to understand their need for God.

"Nannie," Ezra said one Sunday evening after guests had gone home, "there is a great deal of spiritual interest being shown week after week. I have been wondering whether we should have a week of special meetings with salvation messages. What do you think?"

"I agree that some are hungry spiritually. It seems that especially Emma, Greta, and some of their children show interest. Who would bring the messages?" Nannie asked.

"I'm not sure yet," Ezra admitted. "But I'm thinking of having the staff meet some evening next week. I want to get their counsel about this and spend time praying about it together."

"That's a good idea," replied Nannie. "It would be good to hear their perspectives."

When the staff met, Ezra laid out his burden and vision for

the evangelistic meetings and asked for input from the rest of the staff. The Sunday school teachers related their observations about some of the students' interest in the Lord. Those who were involved in home visitation gave names of families that seemed spiritually hungry.

The staff spent time in prayer together, seeking the Lord's direction. Then Ezra spoke again. "I appreciate your responses. From what I hear, you are in support of pursuing this. Someone suggested Johnny Stoltzfus as the speaker for the meetings. I believe he is the man we should ask. He has a heart for the souls of these people, and he preaches in a sincere and convincing way. As far as timing, I would suggest starting tonight in two weeks. Most of the workers in the gold mine who come to church will be on day shift the following week. That way, those who want to come can attend without it interfering with their work schedules."

Thus it was with excitement and some apprehension that the meetings began. Sunday night the building was packed. Johnny preached a powerful message, and the Holy Spirit's work in hearts was evident. When the invitation was given, Emma Stoney, Greta Mosquito and her mother, and some younger girls responded to the call to repent and receive the Lord Jesus Christ into their hearts. There was much rejoicing that night as these souls declared their intentions and prayed to receive Jesus Christ.

Not all were happy about the outcome of events. David Mosquito was aware of his wife's interest in becoming a follower of Jesus, but he was adamantly opposed to her becoming a Mennonite. Before they went to the first evangelistic meeting, David warned his wife that if she became a Mennonite, he would leave her.

That night at the meeting, David heard the message and saw his wife respond to the invitation to receive Christ. In anger David got up and left. Later, after the service was dismissed and Greta had returned home, she found David waiting for her.

"After what I warned you about, why did you respond to the invitation?" he demanded angrily.

"God has been speaking to my heart for a long time," Greta answered softly. "Oh, David, if you only knew how convinced I was about being a sinner and needing Jesus to cleanse and save me, then you would understand why I wanted to respond. David, God has forgiven my sin and has made me clean inside. Jesus has filled me with joy!"

"Well, what you did makes me mad, and just like I said, I am going to leave you," he retorted.

"I feel sorry for you, David," Greta gently responded, "because you won't be happy doing that."

That night Greta went to sleep with a deep peace in her heart. David, however, could not sleep, and at midnight he woke his wife.

"Greta, I am not able to sleep at all," he complained.

"Perhaps we should pray," Greta suggested.

Monday morning came and David went to work. Monday evening he was with his wife at the service. When the invitation was given that night, David responded with several others and made his peace with God. He was a happy man when they went home.

Ezra and Nannie were very grateful and happy as well. They rejoiced that a couple, both man and wife, had given their hearts to the Lord.

Ezra was convinced that people who receive the Lord should

publicly testify to what God was doing in their hearts. Several who responded the first night were willing and publicly declared that they had received Jesus into their hearts. David, however, didn't think he would be able to give a testimony. Maybe, he thought,

^ Ezra preaches in the basement of the Indian School.

when he was a Christian for several months, he might be able to speak in front of the group. Two nights later, however, David was on his feet, happily testifying about what Jesus had done for him.

Many people were burdened for Elijah Stoney, Emma's husband, and prayed for him. One night Elijah attended the service but did not respond to the invitation. Although several men tried to persuade Elijah to surrender his heart to the Lord, he would just shake his head. Elijah wanted nothing to do with what was going on.

Although Emma and several of the children had become

Christians, Elijah would not give in. In fact, he became the chief persecutor against the Christians in his own home. He was short-tempered, uncooperative, and plainly disapproving of the path his wife and children were pursuing. He turned to liquor and friends at the bar for companionship. Elijah began drinking heavily, which made things hard at home. Emma would go out and snare rabbits in order to feed her children. Many hours were spent doing leather beadwork and selling the items to get money to buy food.

One Friday things were getting desperate at home. Emma needed money to get some food for the children. She gathered her courage and went to McDougall's Sawmill where Elijah worked, arriving about the time the workers received their paychecks. When she asked her husband whether she could have the check to buy food for the children, he just stepped around her and walked away. By the next morning the entire paycheck had been spent for liquor.

Emma had almost given up on her husband ever responding to the Gospel when, several months after the special meetings, he surprised her and accompanied her to church. Ezra brought the message that Sunday evening and felt led to give an invitation. Emma was sitting beside her husband on the front row. When the invitation was given, Emma took Elijah's hand and helped him raise it.

Ezra winced inwardly and thought, *Oh, no, don't force him like that.*

However, God was moving in Elijah's heart that night. Later, in the prayer room, Ezra was grateful to hear Elijah pray simply and profoundly, "Lord, I've been away from you for a long time.

Now I want to come to you and follow you."

The way Elijah lived from that night forward demonstrated that he meant what he prayed. He became serious about following Jesus immediately after that prayer.

10
REJOICING IN HEAVEN AND IN RED LAKE

For almost three days a stiff, cold wind howled out of the north while the temperature plunged lower and lower. The birch and poplars were long stripped of their leaves. Only a few broken-off leaf clusters, snagged on lower branches, twitched in the cold blasts of air. The loons and Canada geese had already departed for sunnier climes in the south, while a few diehard ducks still lingered behind.

After breakfast one morning, Ezra buttoned his winter coat and reached for his warm hat.

"Do you need to go out in this weather?" Nannie asked.

"I believe the lake is going to freeze over one of these nights," Ezra responded. "It's high time to get the boat out of the water and turn it upside down for the winter. I know the weather is not very nice, but if I wait much longer, I'll have to use my ice spud and chip the boat out of the lake. With all the wet weather, I kept putting this off. I'm thankful it is not raining or snowing today."

By late morning Ezra's task was completed, and he stepped inside for a few minutes to warm up. Nannie was busy making lunch.

"Would you like some hot tea, dear?" she asked.

"That would be nice, thank you," he replied as he pulled his gloves off and tossed them on the bench. He shrugged out of his coat and backed up to the kitchen stove.

"Ah, that warm stove feels so good. The wind out there really chills a person in a hurry. But you know, the wind is dying down already. If it gets calm by evening, I expect the lake will freeze overnight."

"By the way, dear," Nannie said, "I was thinking of doing something special for your birthday. What do you think of having Elijah and Emma over this evening for a meal?"

"I would like that," Ezra answered. "Have you said anything to them yet?"

"No, I haven't. I wanted to check with you first," Nannie explained.

"I'm eager to hear about their trip north this past summer," Ezra said. "They've shared bits and pieces but not the whole story. Do you want to walk over to Emma's right after lunch and invite them? I'm sure Elijah will still be at work."

"I'll be glad to do that," replied Nannie. "And already I've been thinking about something special to eat."

"What's that?" Ezra wanted to know.

"Well, since it's your birthday meal, I will try to keep it a surprise," she said with a twinkle in her eye. "But I promise it is something you will like."

The winds were calm that evening and the sun had just slipped below the horizon by the time a gentle knock sounded on the Peacheys' door.

"*Biindigen!*" Ezra and Nannie chorused.

"*Miigwech,*" Elijah and Emma answered as they entered. "Thank you for inviting us."

"Happy birthday, Elijah," Ezra said, and then, with mock gravity in his eyes, "And let's see, old timer, how old are you?"

A broad smile wreathed Elijah's face. "Did you forget, Ezra, that we are the same age? Happy birthday to you too."

"*Miigwech,*" answered Ezra. "I was just teasing you a little bit. I forget, what day is your birthday?"

"I really don't know," smiled Elijah. "People have different birthdates for me. I was born up in the bush, and they didn't keep good records back then. Between my parents, the Bearskin village, and the provincial government, three different dates are given. So I certainly don't hold it against you that you can't remember my birthdate."

Soon Nannie told Ezra that the food was ready. They sat down at the table, and Ezra led in prayer, thanking the Lord for the food, for Elijah and Emma, and for the evening of fellowship ahead.

"When I came in, I thought I smelled beaver cooking," Emma commented as the food was passed.

"I wanted to make something special for this birthday meal," Nannie answered. "Ezra and I really enjoy beaver, and I knew both of you are fond of it as well."

"Yes," Elijah agreed. "We do like beaver, but most white people do not seem to like it. You are among the few we know who will eat beaver."

Ezra nodded his head. "Yes," he admitted, "I know some of our people do look down their noses at the very thought of eating beaver, muskrat, or moose nose."

Emma was nodding her head in agreement. "But Nannie, you have sure learned to prepare beaver well. This is very good."

Nannie murmured her thanks and tried to change the subject, not wanting to draw attention to herself. The conversation soon shifted to the cold, calm evening outside with the expected freeze.

When the meal was finished and the dishes washed, Ezra brought up the Stoneys' trip. "I'd be interested in hearing more about your trip north this summer. Can you tell me more about why you took the trip and what happened in your visits?"

"It wasn't very long after my wife and I became Christians that we had a burden on our hearts for friends and relatives back in Bearskin and Fort Severn," Elijah began. "We knew that many of them walked in great darkness, just as we had. What a change the Lord has brought into our lives since we repented and believed! We have a lot of joy in our lives, knowing our sins are forgiven and that we have Jesus's power within us to overcome Satan and sin. It is like we are so full, we want others to learn to know Jesus too. Do you know what I mean?"

Ezra and Nannie didn't say anything but nodded their heads in agreement.

Elijah continued. "That was our desire, and so we prayed about getting time off from work and about the expenses of traveling up north and back. Both of those prayers were answered, so we went ahead with our trip.

"We arrived in Bearskin early enough in the day to have some time for visiting. We hoped and prayed somebody would offer us a place to stay overnight. For several hours though, it felt as if we were not even welcome on our home reserve, almost as though they were angry or fearful of us. It seemed doubtful we would be invited anywhere to sleep. But finally someone invited us to his house."

"Was it hard for you to understand what was going on?" Nannie wanted to know.

"Not really," Emma answered. "I remember how it was when I first heard about Jesus. I, too, was a bit cautious when I first heard the Gospel story."

"And I remember how difficult I was to live with after Emma became a Christian," Elijah added. "I tried to make things hard for those who started living Jesus' way. So I could easily understand how some of them felt. We both knew it might take a while until they were willing to hear our message.

"The next morning we flew up to Fort Severn to see my brother Lazarus. We did not know he had gone to Winnipeg to get hearing aids. I knew for years he had been very hard of hearing, so I was glad he could get them. Still, it was disappointing that we didn't get to see to him. But his wife, Modina, was very interested in hearing of our new life in Christ. She asked us a lot of questions about what it means be a Christian, so we answered the best we knew from the Bible," Elijah explained.

"And," Emma continued, "Elijah asked Modina if she believes she is a sinner according to the Bible. She said yes. Then he asked whether she was truly sorry for her sins and willing to turn from them. Modina was very quiet for a few minutes and then nodded her head. Then I asked if she believed in Jesus who died to redeem her. She told us she understands and believes. Elijah asked her whether she wants to talk to Jesus and invite Him into her heart. We were so happy to help Modina become a follower of Jesus."

"That's wonderful to hear," exclaimed Ezra. "The Bible says there is rejoicing in heaven over one sinner who repents. We know that it is not only us down here in Red Lake who are rejoicing over this good news."

"I am happy for Modina," Nannie said, "and I hope to meet her someday. We need to pray for Lazarus to come to the Lord as well."

They all agreed to pray for Lazarus' salvation, knowing nothing of an unusual request that was heading their way.

11

WE WRESTLE NOT AGAINST FLESH AND BLOOD

"Yum, something smells really good, Nannie," Ezra exclaimed as he came in late one afternoon. What's cooking?"

"Moose meat, onions, carrots, and potatoes," replied Nannie. "I thought you'd be pretty hungry tonight, and I know you like this combination."

After bowing their heads in prayer, they began their evening meal. Little was said until they were almost finished eating.

"I got a letter today concerning some meetings that are going to be held in Deer Lake[1] next month," Ezra said, breaking the silence. "They want me to come and speak on spiritualism. That is a pertinent subject in this culture."

"It sure is," agreed Nannie. "When something comes up along that line in conversation with the ladies, it gets pretty quiet. It

---

[1] One of Northern Light Gospel Mission's church-planting outposts was located in Deer Lake, about 110 miles north of Red Lake. NLGM frequently sponsored conferences for the native churches that dealt with relevant issues, and sometimes MIC workers were invited to speak.

seems they are afraid to talk of such things."

"Most of them have far more experience with spirit manifestations than we do," replied Ezra. "But as I was thinking about how to approach this topic, God led me to speak first about my own experience. Remember what happened that night in our bedroom a couple years ago?"

"I do," Nannie said without hesitation.

"That night as I wondered why an evil presence was in our bedroom, I became aware that my involvement with water witching was holding me back in some areas of ministry. Since we renounced those things, it seems we've had greater freedom and power and wisdom to deal with issues of spiritualism here."

Nannie added, "Remember when we first came to Red Lake and would hear drums beating in the evening? It seemed there was something evil connected with the drumming."

"Yes," replied Ezra, "there are some other incidents like that too that I might speak about at the meetings. Let's pray that God would direct my thoughts, and that I might speak the truth in love."

When Ezra got up and introduced his subject some weeks later, he could tell instantly that every ear was listening. He began by telling the audience of his own involvement with spiritualism.

"When I was twelve years old, I observed two things in my culture back in Pennsylvania that are referred to as 'water smelling,' or 'water witching.' I observed a man walking, holding a forked tree branch in his hands. When he got above an underground source of water, the branch bent downward. Then I also saw a man using a pendulum to determine how far below the surface the water was located. Those things were interesting to me. I never gave it much thought, though, why it worked for some people and didn't work for others.

"One day when I had a little spare time, I got a forked branch and began walking around with it. Sure enough, when I got to a certain spot, the branch pulled down. I didn't have a pendulum, but I did have a piece of metal on the end of a string. When I held it over the spot where the branch pulled down, the piece of metal started to swing. It swung seventy-two times. Two men were working nearby, and I told them what I had found. They looked at each other in amazement before saying that there used to be a well in that exact location, and the water was eighty feet down."

Some of the people at Deer Lake were looking intently at Ezra, solemn looks on their faces. The rest were staring at the floor, but they, too, were listening as Ezra continued.

"When we moved to Red Lake, we would hear the drums beating some nights. Nannie and I never went to investigate or watch. Something about those drums gave us unrest inside. It was like something arguing with the Holy Spirit of God who lives inside those who receive Jesus Christ into their hearts. I could tell there was conflict between the power of the drums and the power of the Holy Spirit."

Ezra went on. "Later, the people who owned the one drum moved away. For some reason, they left their drum and drumsticks behind. A man brought those items to our house and asked us to keep them for him. So those things were in our home for a while. The man who brought them also moved away and did not come back. We were having some spiritual problems in our home—problems with bad attitudes—and we wondered whether that drum might have something to do with it. I was also dealing with a situation where someone was involved with evil spirits, and I soon discovered I lacked wisdom and power to make any progress in that situation. Then one night I suddenly woke up from a deep sleep. It seemed that something evil was in our bedroom. There was a terrible, oppressive spirit present. I knew instantly it was an evil spirit; there was no question about that."

Ezra noticed that some in the audience were staring at him with fearful expressions on their faces. One man was visibly uncomfortable. Ezra breathed a silent prayer for strength and utterance to say what God wanted him to say.

"I thought of the verse in 1 John 4:3. 'And every spirit that confesseth not that Jesus Christ is come in the flesh is not of God: and this is that spirit of antichrist, whereof ye have heard that it should come; and even now already is it in the world.' So I tried to confess out loud that Jesus Christ IS come in the flesh. I couldn't get the words out. It seemed my tongue was stuck in my mouth. But finally I managed to say it out loud. And just that quick, everything was clear and there was peace in the bedroom. The oppressive spirit was gone.

"As I lay there afterward, I found myself questioning what had happened. Was it real or was it just a dream? I wasn't sure.

"But the next morning my wife said to me, 'You talked in your sleep last night.'

" 'Oh!' I said. 'What did I say?'

" 'You said, "Jesus Christ is come in the flesh." '

"So brothers and sisters, I knew for sure that what I experienced was real. And I knew for sure that I needed to renounce water witching for what it was. So I did. The drum and drumsticks were also burned. And in the time since then, God has been so gracious to give wisdom and power when the need arises.

"Some of you have told me things that have happened to people you know. I know some of you may be afraid to even speak of things concerning spiritualism. Others are aware that we need to speak of these things, however uncomfortable it might be.

"I know of a husband and his wife who both had an interest in coming to the Lord, but they both also had a weakness for strong drink. At a Christmas party, they got drunk and did things they should not have done. Trouble came into their marriage. So this husband went to his father, who had a spirit helper, the caribou. The man asked his father for some strong medicine to make his wife love him again. At this same time, the husband again expressed to me his desire to get right with God, but he said he wasn't quite ready yet. That was the last I spoke with him. He disappeared, and a relative asked whether I had seen anything of the man. I hadn't, and I also wondered what happened to him. Not long afterward, the man's dead body was found floating in the lake. His watch and billfold were missing. There are unanswered questions about those circumstances to this day.

"Magnus James[2] told me personally about a man making contact with evil spirits in a shaking-teepee ceremony. Magnus said that when the Hudson Bay store manager heard about it, he laughed at the man and told him he was simply shaking the teepee

---

[2] Magnus James was a Christian man from MacDowell Lake, a neighboring reserve. He was well-known and respected by many in attendance at Deer Lake.

himself. So the man who did the ceremony challenged the store manager to fasten the teepee so that it couldn't be shaken. The store manager pounded some stakes in the ground. He brought new rope and tied the teepee down so firmly that he was sure no human could shake it. Then, when the ceremony began, the teepee began to shake. It shook so violently that those new ropes tore apart. It was pretty convincing evidence to the manager that there was some strong power behind what happened.

"Sometimes," Ezra continued, "a man will use this power to make others afraid of him. When others are afraid, he can ask for this or that and they will give it to him as a present. They are scared that if they don't give a gift, something bad will happen to them. People with this kind of evil power often use it to gain an advantage over others.

"In Acts chapter 8, the Bible tells us about a man who had this kind of evil power. Simon used sorcery and bewitched the people of Samaria. He used his power to make himself look like he was a great person. Verses 10 and 11 read, 'To whom they all gave heed, from the least to the greatest, saying, This man is the great power of God. And to him they had regard, because that of a long time he had bewitched them with sorceries.'

"Simon used power from Satan to control the people around him. He used this power so effectively that the people feared him. They paid attention to what he said. They were afraid to go against the commands he gave. They were even cautious about saying anything against him for fear he would use his power against them. Why? Because he had held them captive to his power for a long time. He would use ceremonies, potions, curses, omens, and suchlike to hold them in fear. And the people viewed the power he had as coming from God. We know for certain, however, that this power was not from God. The Bible is very clear that these kinds of manifestations are not of God, but of the devil.

"Magnus James's grandson, Elijah James, tells of a group of men from MacDowell Lake who went toward Manitoba to hunt moose. They met up with another group of men from Manitoba. One of the men from Manitoba had been told that Ronald Whitefish[3] from MacDowell Lake had power. He and the men with him gave some gifts and tobacco to Ronald and asked him to make it rain. They had been sent out by the forestry service to fight a fire burning in the area, but they really didn't want to fight the fire. So Ronald agreed to try to make it rain. That night, not only did it rain, but it also snowed. It took care of the fire. Those men from Manitoba were really amazed at the power Ronald possessed."

As Ezra continued his message, he turned to a number of passages in the Bible where God gave clear instruction not to be involved with divination, enchanters, witches, charmers, familiar spirits, wizards, or those who seek to contact the dead. He showed that such things are an abomination to God and should not be part of the Christian's life. Ezra gave examples from Scripture of the sad end of those who dabbled in such things. He spoke from Acts 19 about the blessing people received when they confessed and repented of their involvement in these occult activities.

Ezra lifted his eyes and scanned the group before him. "There is one more story I need to tell you. It is about Fred.[4] Fred and

[3] Pseudonym used.
[4] Pseudonym used.

his wife made a commitment to the Lord. They began to attend church regularly, but then they started to slip back into their old ways. Fred began saying things that were not true. Something seemed to grip him. So one day I asked Fred, 'Do you have a medicine bag?' He admitted he did. I told him, 'As long as you have that medicine bag, you will never be successful in the Christian life. You need to get rid of it.' Fred told me his uncle had given it to him. The medicine bag gave him lots of power, and he would not give it up.

"Fred's life had a sad ending. He is not the only person who tried standing with one foot in the devil's canoe and the other foot in Jesus' canoe. That will never work! In the natural world, someone who tries to stand with one foot in one canoe and the other foot in another canoe is soon going to fall into the lake and get wet. In the spiritual world, he falls into sin and is defeated.

"Light and darkness do not mix. They cannot dwell together. One or the other has to go. Paul admonished the Christians at Ephesus to have nothing to do with the activities of darkness but rather to reprove or expose them for what they are. James teaches that we need to submit ourselves to God. We are to resist the devil, and he will flee from us. We do not need to be afraid of the devil, for God's power in us is greater than the power of Satan.

"Where we have walked in darkness, let us come to God for cleansing. Where we have been fearful of the devil and what he might do, let us come boldly before God's throne of grace. Let us ask Him for power to live fearlessly for Jesus and then proclaim to others the power He has to deliver us from all evil."

After the close of the service, there was a time of quiet

conversation among a number of the men who stayed behind. Ezra visited with several of the native believers. Before leaving, a younger man came to Ezra to greet him and discuss a few thoughts.

"My father and I listened carefully to what you had to say tonight," he began. "When the service was over, I asked my father what he thinks about what we heard. His answer was, 'We don't talk about those things.' "

"Why is that?" Ezra questioned. "Do people not talk about these things because they fear the evil spirits and are afraid of what might happen to them if they speak out about God's protection and power to overcome evil?"

The young man nodded his head. "I think that is the reason my father's generation has been silent about this topic. After my father's comment about the message, I told him that we need to talk about this. Thank you for speaking so openly and plainly tonight."

12
GO HOME AND TELL

After David and Greta Mosquito became Christians, they had a burden for the souls of their families and friends in Bearskin Lake. That burden became more important to them than the comfortable living David was providing by his steady job at the gold mine. They were determined to move back, even though they knew they would face significant opposition in Bearskin because of their decision to follow the Lord.

"Have you heard from your father lately?" Greta asked David one day as they were packing their possessions.

"No, I have not heard from him for a long time. When I started writing about giving our hearts to the Lord, he stopped answering my letters. I have heard several reports that the people of Bearskin don't want anything to do with our new religion. They don't even want to hear about it. Some of our friends here have warned us that it will be very difficult to move back, but we are natives of Bearskin; we can go and live there."

"It may take a while until they see that what we have is for real.

Oh, I long so much for them to find the peace and joy we have found in the Lord," Greta said. "Do you think they even know we are moving back?"

"I wrote to my father last week telling him we are coming and planning to move back into our house. He hasn't replied, so I'm not sure what to expect when we show up."

When David and Greta and their family landed at the Bearskin settlement, David's father and brother came down to the plane and helped them unload. Then they turned to David. "We are glad you came, but we don't want to hear anything about your religion."

"Miigwech," David began. "I did not come to preach. But when an opportunity comes, I will tell what the Lord has done for me."

With these words as their motto and goal, David and Greta entered back into life at Bearskin Lake. At first they felt coldness from their neighbors. People seemed to try to avoid meeting them on the pathways around the settlement. David and Greta knew they were being watched closely to see how they would respond to the chilly reception.

A few months later David attended a conference at Pikangikum that he had been invited to. Henry Hostetler from Northern Light Gospel Mission flew in to pick him up. When they were airborne, David turned to Henry and asked, "Did you notice that nobody came to see me off?"

Henry nodded. "Yes, I did notice. It seemed a bit unusual. Why do you suppose that was?"

"Bearskin is very closed to the Gospel at this point. That was made clear to us when we returned from Red Lake. We have been told to keep quiet about our religion."

"Are you in danger living there?" Henry wanted to know.

"I wouldn't say we're in danger," David replied slowly, "but I don't go out at night."

"Well, I want to encourage you to keep living for the Lord," Henry said. "Be faithful to God and His Word. It may take some time for people to see the difference Jesus makes in your life. I hope this conference will be an encouragement to you and the other Christians who are coming."

After the conference, David returned to his wife and children at Bearskin. As the months passed, the people began to respect the Mosquitos for what they believed and how they were living. They observed these new believers trying to live out Jesus' teachings right before their eyes.

^ The David Mosquito family.

About a year and a half later, a six-week Bible school was planned at the Red Lake Indian School, and David and Greta wanted to attend. They found a free ride down to the railroad station at Savant Lake. David called Ezra to inform him that they were coming by train to Red Lake Road. Ezra drove the 160 kilometers down from Red Lake and picked them up.

The Bible school proved to be a blessing to students and staff alike. Various mission and native leaders taught the classes. It was a time of spiritual instruction and growth. When Bible school was over, David began working again at the gold mine in Red Lake until just before freeze-up that fall. Then David and Greta returned to Bearskin, this time to a much warmer reception. David was able to find work there that winter, and people appreciated his good work habits and responsible manner. Still, people were reluctant to hear the Gospel message.

"You know, Greta," David said as he sat down at the table one December evening. "It sure is nice to feel accepted for who we are here at Bearskin. But I am having little success in finding people willing to hear me talk about Jesus. As soon as I try to turn a conversation to those things, people change the subject."

"My husband, don't be discouraged," Greta told him. "Jesus never promised it would be easy to win souls. We have already experienced persecution that the Bible talks about. You have been faithful in sharing with those who will listen for a little bit. The Lord will give the increase in His time."

13
NEW LIFE FOR LAZARUS

Normally Elijah was laid back and taciturn, but not this time. When he knocked on Ezra's door one evening, he was eager to talk.

"I received a letter from my brother Lazarus today," he blurted out. "He was sorry that he missed us when Emma and I went to Fort Severn several months ago. But he wrote in his letter that he wants me to come again, and you are to come along. What do you think about that?"

"Did he say why he wants me to come along?" Ezra wanted to know.

"Not really," Elijah replied, "but I wonder whether it has something to do with Modina becoming a Christian."

"Maybe the letter indicates that God is answering our prayers for Lazarus' salvation. Of course, we don't know for sure, but maybe he is wanting what his wife has found," Ezra pondered out loud.

Ezra was quiet for a few minutes as he thought through these things.

"I am certainly willing to go with you, Elijah," Ezra spoke up.

"When are you thinking of going?"

"I don't have to work Saturday or Sunday on the garbage truck, and I think I might be able to get Monday off. Would it work to go this coming weekend?"

"Who would be going?" Ezra inquired.

"I was thinking you and I could fly to Bearskin. Maybe we could take David Mosquito along as far as Fort Severn. Do you think you could use the PA-12 for this trip?"

Ezra thought awhile before he spoke.

"Perhaps I could, but right now I am not comfortable with taking it to Fort Severn in this winter weather. The daylight hours are shorter this time of year, and the PA-12 flies pretty slow. I think we should check with NLGM to see if their Cessna 180 would be available. That cruises nearly sixty miles an hour faster."

"Would you fly it?" Elijah inquired.

"No, I would ask Whitey Hostetler. He has much more experience with the 180 and winter flying than I do," admitted Ezra. "But the Cessna holds four people, so your idea of picking up David Mosquito in Bearskin should still work."

Jay Wendell Hostetler, usually known as Whitey, had moved to Red Lake in 1958 to work for NLGM as a pilot and mechanic. Eight years later, he started his own business, Red Lake Seaplane Service. The business was commonly referred to as "Whitey's Hangar" or just "Whitey's." It was located across the bay from NLGM's headquarters and served commercial aircraft as well as mission planes.

Ezra contacted Irwin Schantz about using the Cessna and proceeded to work out other details with Whitey in preparation for

Saturday's flight. One way or another, they needed to be back home Monday evening because of Elijah's job.

At first light Saturday morning, Ezra and Elijah walked out onto Howey Bay where the 180 was warming up. Whitey shut off the motor as they approached and climbed out. "Good morning, men," he drawled. "She's warmed up and ready to go."

While the two men climbed in and fastened their seat belts, Whitey walked around the plane and gave each ski a hard kick. This cracked the ice bond where the ski had frozen fast to the lake surface. With that, Whitey climbed in and started the engine. When all was clear, he gunned the engine briefly to begin taxiing toward the town-end of the snow-packed runway. After visually confirming that no other planes were landing or taking off, Whitey lined up with the runway and pushed the throttle to full power. The 230 HP Continental engine howled loudly as its propeller bit into the frosty air and pulled the plane rapidly down the runway. When the proper speed was reached, Whitey eased back on the control yoke, and the Cessna climbed briskly into the early morning light. Whitey adjusted the throttle to cruising speed and banked the airplane to the correct compass heading for Bearskin Lake.

Seventy-five miles short of Bearskin, they encountered bad weather. It was snowing heavily, and visibility was growing poorer by the minute. Whitey descended lower and lower to keep the trees below within sight. He knew the danger of pressing on in white-out conditions. More than one pilot had crashed when flying over a snow-covered lake during a snowstorm, unable to distinguish between the blinding snow and the surface of the lake. When Whitey voiced his opinion that they should land at Weagamow (Round) Lake, Ezra was relieved. They landed without incident and spent the rest of Saturday and all of Sunday with Christian friends there.

By Monday morning the skies had cleared sufficiently, so they took off and flew to Bearskin Lake. There they were told that David Mosquito and another man were out trapping on a lake some miles to the south. With that information, the three men decided that for time's sake, they needed to press on to Fort Severn without David.

The weather was windy, stormy, and cold as Whitey finally settled the skis onto the frozen Severn River. When Elijah and Ezra climbed up the bank from the river, people from the settlement gathered around. They knew Elijah, but they wondered who Ezra was.

When Lazarus heard it was Ezra who had come with his brother, he welcomed them. "Please come up to my house," he invited, nodding his head in that direction.

"Miigwech," Elijah and Ezra said as they followed Lazarus. "We won't be able to stay more than a couple hours. We need to get back to Red Lake before dark."

When the men were seated, Lazarus began asking questions about the change in his wife since she had given her heart to the Lord. He spoke in Oji-Cree, so someone interpreted for Ezra. "What does it mean to be a Christian?" he asked, looking intently at Ezra. "Something is different about Modina since Elijah and Emma were here a few months ago."

Ezra answered, "A Christian is one who turns from sin and

chooses to follow Jesus' path."

Lazarus followed with another question. "How does a person know what Jesus' path looks like?"

"God has given us His Word, the Bible," Ezra explained. "It tells us how Jesus wants us to live. God's Word explains what it means to turn away from wickedness and unbelief. It also instructs us how to live right in the sight of God. Lazarus, when you walk on a trail in the bush, you sometimes come to a fork in the trail. Can you picture that in your mind?"

Lazarus nodded.

"How do you decide which trail to take?" Ezra went on.

Lazarus pondered a few moments and then replied, "I take the trail that goes in the direction I want to go."

"When a man becomes a Christian," Ezra explained, "he chooses the trail that Jesus wants for him instead of taking the trail that he wants to walk. Perhaps an illustration will help.

"If someone here at Fort Severn does something mean to you, it's as if you are standing at a fork in the trail. The one fork represents what you feel like doing—getting even, becoming angry, or doing something mean back to him. The other fork is explained in the Bible. God's Word teaches followers of Jesus to return good for evil. Jesus commands us to love our enemies, to do good to those who do wrong to us. So when a man becomes a Christian, he is no longer his own boss. Jesus becomes his *Kitchi Ogimaa.*"[1]

"I think I understand that," Lazarus said, "but how does one become a Christian?"

---

[1] *Big leader* or *big boss.* Pronounced KĬT chĭ OH gĭ mah.

Using simple words and illustrations, Ezra went on to explain how a person needs to come to the place where he acknowledges he is a sinner. Ezra spoke about the need to develop an attitude of repentance in the heart, a feeling of being truly sorry for sin and being willing to turn from it. Ezra told Lazarus about the Gospel, the good news that God sent His Son Jesus to shed His blood and die for our sins, and that those who receive Jesus into their hearts are forgiven and made into new people in Christ. He explained how God gives His children His precious Holy Spirit to live inside their hearts and help them know which path God wants them to take.

Finally Ezra asked, "Lazarus, did you ever become a Christian?"

"I have been waiting for you to come," Lazarus replied. "Ever since I saw the change that came in my wife, I have wanted to know how I can get what she has. Yes, I want to receive Jesus as *ogimaa*[2] of my life."

Then Lazarus prayed. He confessed his sin and asked Jesus Christ to come into his heart. Ezra and Elijah also prayed, thanking God for the work He was doing in Lazarus' heart and home and for giving them the opportunity to share the Gospel. What a time of rejoicing!

Modina prepared food for the men, and soon it was time for them to head home again. By now the gusty wind had picked up. Looking out across the river, Ezra saw the wind-sculpted waves of snow and knew it would be a rough takeoff.

They buckled themselves in as the engine warmed up. *I'm*

---

[2] *Leader* or *boss*.

grateful that Whitey is flying, Ezra thought as the wind buffeted the wings. *He can handle it.*

"Ready?" asked Whitey. He pointed the Cessna into the wind and opened the throttle. The dashboard shook as the airplane's skis bounced over the rough surface of the river ice. As they neared takeoff speed, Ezra braced himself as he saw they were bearing down on a larger drift of snow. When they went up over the snow bank, they didn't come back down; they were airborne.

Whitey flew, and Ezra helped navigate to the lake where David Mosquito was trapping. They landed and had a brief visit with David, telling him how they had hoped that he could have gone along to Fort Severn. David rejoiced with Ezra and Elijah to hear that Lazarus had given his heart to the Lord. With mutual wishes for the Lord's blessing, the three men left David, and soon their plane was heading for Red Lake and home.

14
BACK TO BEARSKIN

"I had a close call today," Elijah told his wife one afternoon when he came home from work.

"What happened?" Emma wondered.

"I wasn't paying attention like I should have," he began. "I was concentrating on loading the garbage truck and didn't check to see whether cars were coming. With my poor hearing, I couldn't hear the traffic either. Without thinking, I stepped out into traffic and almost got run over by a car. Thankfully, the driver swerved and missed me."

"Praise the Lord that you weren't hit!" Emma exclaimed. "But isn't this the third or fourth time this has happened?"

"Yes, it is," Elijah said soberly. "And that's what bothers me. I can't figure out why I don't remember to be more careful since my one ear and one eye are basically useless. I guess I just forgot. And that's not all that happened today. One of the Red Lake town officials talked to me about this just before I came home. They've heard about my close calls and are concerned that I might get hit or even killed. He told me that several of the town officials even talked to Ezra about these incidents. Has Nannie said anything to you?"

"No, she hasn't," Emma replied. "What are they talking about?"

"They wanted to know if Ezra had any advice for them," Elijah explained. "It has come to the point that they want to retire me before something worse happens. That is what the official wanted to talk to me about. What do you think about that?"

"I don't know, Elijah," Emma said. "How would you earn money for us to live?"

"The officer said the town would pay me a pension, and according to what he told me, we should be able to live on that amount. They want me to retire in a few weeks."

"That soon? What will you do after retiring?" Emma asked.

"I have been thinking for some time now that the Lord may be calling us to live at Bearskin," Elijah said thoughtfully. "Ever since we gave our hearts to the Lord, I have had a burden for our unsaved friends and relatives back home. David and Greta have gone back some time ago. Together with them, maybe we can win more souls for Christ there. Do you think God may be directing us back to Bearskin?"

"It certainly would appear that way. I would be happy to move back home. When would we go?" Emma was excited.

"Is there anything to keep us from moving back when I am finished with my job in a few weeks?" Elijah asked.

"I guess not," Emma answered. "It will be hard to say goodbye to Ezra and Nannie and all our friends here. This place and these people will always be special because this is where we found the Lord."

BACK TO BEARSKIN

Ezra and Nannie had mixed feelings about the Stoneys' move back to Bearskin. Along with the rest of the church, Ezra and Nannie would sorely miss the Stoneys at Red Lake. Elijah and Emma had lived out their faith, and those who knew them saw the change God had wrought in their lives. Although they would be greatly missed, Ezra and Nannie also understood the boost and blessing the Stoney family would be to the David Mosquito family back at Bearskin. It appeared that Red Lake's loss would be Bearskin's gain, and the Peacheys blessed Elijah and Emma in their plans to move.

Several weeks later, after goodbyes and farewells were exchanged, Elijah and Emma and their family boarded a chartered airplane that flew them home to Bearskin Lake. God blessed their Christian testimony, and they became an important part of the small but growing group of believers there.

15
LESSONS FROM THE TRAPLINE

During their time in the North, Ezra and his sons spent time trapping. One of the reasons Ezra did this was to better understand something that was so common to the people to whom they were ministering.

When Ezra preached at the church in Red Lake or in other native settlements, he would often use lessons and illustrations to which his audience could relate. He often referred to things he had learned on the trapline. Here is one message he preached based on his experiences in trapping.

"This evening, I would like to talk about several things I have learned on the trapline," Ezra began. "As a boy growing up in Pennsylvania, I trapped muskrats in the streams near my home. I would set a leg trap in the water where a muskrat had tunneled back under the bank of the stream. The trap would be anchored with a stake in deeper water when possible. When the muskrat stepped on the trap, the jaw would snap on its leg and hold it from swimming off. As it tried to move around, it would drown in the deeper water. Each morning I checked the traps, and when I found a muskrat, I would take it home, skin it, and sell the fur.

"My sons and I are learning to trap up here in the bush. It is something we enjoy doing. A few years ago a man gave me the use of his trapline near Red Lake, and later he sold me the trapping rights. Trapping has helped me understand something that has been a way of life for many of your families. You know the feeling of thankfulness that comes from finding a nice fisher or a large beaver in the trap. A large beaver pelt will bring enough money to buy a lot of flour and evaporated milk. Fishers are a rarer species, and when you catch one, you've earned enough money to buy your wife a warm coat.

"Many of you know far more about trapping than I do, and you've taught me about trapping. One man explained to me recently how he makes a teepee set when he's trapping. I had never heard of it before. But when he told me how he does it, it made sense. As I studied how he made his teepee set, God showed me some lessons about life and temptation that we can learn from this method of trapping.

"In trapping, there are two characters: the trapper and the animal. The trapper wants to catch the animal, but the animal wants to stay far away from him. The trapper is the animal's adversary.

"There are some spiritual parallels. The trapper is like the devil and we, the people, are like the animals. Some of us are big and round and fat like the beaver. Others of us are slender like the fox. But all of us, whatever size, whatever the color of our skin, have an adversary—the devil. He is trying to make sets to catch us. He uses many tricks to catch men and women and lead them to destruction. One of Satan's tricks is to make people comfortable.

"In the summer, the trapper builds a teepee in a place he plans to trap in the winter. When a marten first sees the teepee, it might be careful about getting too near this strange structure. After all, it is something new in the area. But when the teepee is there day after day, week after week, month after month, it no longer seems out of place. The marten gets used to seeing it there all the time and no longer is cautious about going near it. What the marten does not know is that his adversary, the trapper, built the teepee with the purpose of harvesting the marten's valuable fur. Animals cannot think and reason like people can.

"God tells us in Ephesians 6:11 to put on the whole armor of God so that we can stand against the trickery of the devil. Satan tries to get us to be comfortable in a setting where it is easy to sin. At first, like the marten, we think something may seem out of place. But in time, it all becomes familiar, and we lose some of our caution.

"When trapping season is drawing closer, the trapper hangs some fish high in the teepee. The marten smells the fish and wants to eat it. Maybe it hasn't eaten for several days. Maybe it has already eaten but wants more food to put on fat for winter. So the marten climbs up a pole in the teepee to eat the fish hanging there. It is an easy meal. As the weeks pass by, the marten may expect there will be a meal of fish waiting for it in the teepee whenever he passes that way. In fact, the little animal may spend more and more time in the area where he finds such easy and tasty meals.

"Satan uses bait too. He uses bait that appeals to our sinful desires. He often places it in places where the person has become quite comfortable. After taking Satan's bait a number of times, the sin doesn't seem so bad after all. In fact, it becomes something the person looks forward to doing more and more. The Bible tells us in James 1:14 that every man is tempted when he is drawn away of his own lust and enticed. The devil hangs bait that appeals to man's desire for what God forbids. The first time man sinned in the Bible, Satan made the bait look so desirable and so attractive. It became so appealing that Eve picked and ate the fruit from this only tree in the Garden of Eden that God had forbidden Adam and Eve to eat of. That is the way our adversary, the devil, works. God has given many good and pleasant things for our nourishment and enjoyment, but the devil baits us with things that God has forbidden. Just as the marten does not think about what the bait in the teepee is leading him into, many people go after the devil's bait, unaware that they are in the process of getting trapped or snared.

"At the time of year when furs are in prime condition and the marten has been coming to the teepee regularly, the trapper fastens a body-gripping trap on the pole. The only way the marten can get to the fish above is to climb up headfirst through those extra 'sticks' that have appeared on the pole. It is the last meal that marten will try to eat. When it trips the trigger wire, the jaws snap tightly around its body and the marten can no longer breathe. Within a couple minutes the animal is dead.

"So it is with people. The time comes when people are 'hooked.' They, too, are caught and cannot get away. They have been taken captive by Satan. They have yielded too many times and are unable on their own to break free of the trap the devil has set for them.

The Apostle Paul wrote to Timothy about gently teaching those who have been taken captive by Satan.

"With the marten, when the trap snaps, his end is sure. When the devil snares a person, he traps them to destroy them. The devil wants to make sure the people he captures go to hell, where they will suffer for all eternity.

"We are nearing the end of today's trapline lessons. We must remain attentive lest the tricky devil tempts us to become comfortable in wicked situations. May we always be aware that the sinful things that tempt us are being used to draw us away from God's house and into the devil's teepee where he can trap us. My hope and prayer is that none of us will be caught in Satan's trap.

"And when you see people who have been caught in Satan's snare, gently teach them. By the power of God, they can be delivered from the snare of the devil, for God is more powerful than Satan. When someone is caught in the devil's snare, it is not the end. There is still hope if those people are willing to be freed."

16

BAPTISMAL TRIP TO FORT SEVERN

It was September, and there were many reminders that winter was on the way. Already several hard frosts had finished off the gardens, and moose hunting season lay just ahead. It was an especially enjoyable time of the year. Mornings often dawned clear and cold; a warm jacket felt good. On such afternoons during Indian summer, the coat could be laid aside for a few hours. Fall weather in the North can be unpredictable, with a cold rain squall followed shortly by bright sunshine. As one old timer told Ezra and Nannie, "If you don't like the weather in the fall, just wait fifteen minutes." During this changeable weather, Ezra often chuckled as he remembered that saying.

"Nannie, have you noticed how much earlier it is getting dark in the evenings?" Ezra asked as he spooned the last bit of soup from his bowl one evening.

"Yes, I have," she replied. "It's amazing how quickly it has changed from those long summer evenings."

"I've been thinking about Lazarus and his wife Modina and their request to be baptized," Ezra continued. "I believe they understand what it means to be Christians and to be numbered publicly with the believers. With her poor health, I've been wondering today whether I should try to fly in for their baptism before the lakes begin freezing up. What do you think?"

"That would seem wise to me, Ezra," Nannie agreed. "If you don't go before the lakes begin to freeze, you might have to wait several more weeks until the ice is thick enough to land on. And with Modina's physical condition, baptizing sooner rather than later would seem better."

"Let's pray about it and sleep over it," Ezra suggested. "If it still seems tomorrow morning that this is what God wants us to do, then I think we should proceed."

After breakfast the next morning, Ezra read a portion of Scripture and shared a few thoughts from the reading. Again, they laid their request for wisdom and direction before the Lord in fervent prayer.

As they arose from prayer, Ezra turned to his wife. "Honey, I believe the Lord wants me to go to Fort Severn as soon as possible. What are your thoughts?"

"I agree," Nannie replied. "I'm always happy to have you at home, and I know you like being here too. The boys and I will miss you. Nonetheless, I appreciate your willingness to assist these dear souls in their spiritual journeys. Will you go alone?"

"I was thinking about picking up Elijah and taking him along," Ezra said. "It would be meaningful to him to be present for his brother's baptism. Also, I'm sure it would be a blessing to Lazarus and his wife for Elijah to be there."

"So you will fly to Bearskin alone?" Nannie wondered.

"Yes, I would probably take along a load of gas and leave some of it at Bearskin to refuel on the way home," Ezra explained. "I would drop off the gas and pick up Elijah and go on to Fort Severn. It will be a big day of flying for me, but it seems feasible."

"Well, dear," Nannie said, "you've told me often that you will not take chances when situations aren't safe. I appreciate that you're cautious. May God bless and keep you. When do you plan to leave?"

"I'd like to go this Saturday, Lord willing. That way Elijah and I can spend the Lord's Day at Fort Severn." Ezra sounded excited.

On Saturday morning, Ezra awoke to the sound of wind-lashing rain against the windows of the mission house. When it was light enough to see outside, he knew he was not going anywhere in such conditions. White caps on the lake and low clouds in the sky convinced him it would not be wise to fly that day. In bush pilot's lingo, the weather was "out." He would have to go on Sunday.

Early Sunday morning, Ezra stowed what few belongings he needed into the back of the PA-12. With the hand pump that was kept inside the plane, he pumped out each float compartment section to remove any water that might have seeped in. When he was satisfied that a section was empty, he replaced that section's stopper and moved on to the next section. Finally, when both floats were pumped out, he made sure both wing tanks were full of fuel and that no water was in the fuel lines. The engine oil was on the full mark and the flight controls seemed to be working properly. He untied from the dock, pushed the plane away and climbed in. The engine started on the first try. He waved goodbye to Nannie and the boys as the spinning propeller pulled the plane away from the dock.

After several minutes of taxiing and warming up the engine, Ezra pushed the rudder pedal to turn the plane into the wind. Then he slid the throttle steadily and firmly to full throttle. As the plane picked up speed, he gently maneuvered the stick until he was "on step."[1] Picking up a bit more speed, he lifted one wing to break the float on that side free of the water. Then the other wing was lifted, and Ezra was airborne.

Two and a half hours later, Ezra set his craft down on the choppy waters of Bearskin Lake. Elijah met him at the dock.

"*Boozhoo*, Elijah," called out Ezra as he swung the airplane's door open.

"*Boozhoo*, Ezra," Elijah returned. "It's a nice day."

"I agree," Ezra said. "The weather is sure better than yesterday. Thank you for catching the plane and helping me dock. Did you get my message inviting you along to Fort Severn for the baptism of Lazarus and Modina?"

"Yes, I did. I was thinking you might even come yesterday. But when you didn't show up, I kept listening for a plane today. I'm happy you made it safely. Why don't you come up to our house and rest a bit?"

After a short visit, with a little food and tea, Ezra refueled the airplane, and the men took off. They arrived in Fort Severn two hours later.

The community of Fort Severn had a church building, and there

---

[1] "On step" is a term used by bush pilots to describe the phase of a float plane's acceleration where sufficient speed has been attained to lift the plane higher in the water. When a plane is on step, the front portions of the floats are largely clear of the water and the tapered, stepped-up rear portions of the floats are all that remain in contact with the water.

were a number of people in the settlement who professed faith in God. However, there was no pastor serving the church at the time.

Lazarus wanted to have his baptism in the church so that interested people could come and observe. Modina's health, however, was so poor that she was unable to walk to the community church and be baptized there. So they decided to have two separate baptismal services.

The baptismal service for Lazarus in the church was held first. Because many in the audience did not understand much English and Ezra did not speak Oji-Cree, he spoke through an interpreter.

Ezra spoke about the new birth and the importance of baptism to the almost two dozen people who had gathered. Ezra told of his meeting with Lazarus and Modina earlier that fall for Bible instruction. Lazarus gave testimony to the change Jesus Christ had brought into his heart, and then Ezra baptized him. Lazarus became the first Christian baptized in Fort Severn who chose to identify with the Mennonite church.

Ezra was glad that Elijah could be along to encourage his brother and witness what took place that evening. Several of the others who were present had questions about what they had observed.

Following Lazarus' baptism in the church building, a much smaller group gathered in Lazarus' home. Only Lazarus, Modina, their daughter, and two other people joined Elijah and Ezra in the small two-room house.

Ezra spoke again, more briefly than before, and Modina gave testimony of peace with God and a desire to be identified with her husband as a believer. Their daughter interpreted throughout the brief service, and Modina was baptized.

All in all, it had been a strenuous but rewarding day for Ezra. Two more souls had publicly sealed their testimony for the Lord in Christian baptism. It was with a grateful heart that Ezra lay down to sleep that night.

New life grew from the seed that Elijah and Emma planted in Fort Severn. Over the next four years, several other souls also received the Lord and were baptized and added to the church. God was giving the increase.

17

AN UNEXPECTED CAMPING TRIP

"Goose season opens tomorrow," Lazarus informed Ezra the next morning. "Since you are here already, would you consider staying for a goose hunt?"

"That sounds like an idea worth considering," answered Ezra. He took another piece of bannock and spread it with jam as he thought about the possibilities. Ezra had often heard about the excellent goose hunting at Fort Severn. This was a rare opportunity to hunt geese here without incurring the expense of a special trip to this town in the Far North. Nannie knew that whenever he left home to fly to the northern reserves, there was uncertainty as to when he would return, and she wouldn't mind if he spent some time goose hunting with these men. A few days could be spared in his schedule, but he wasn't sure Elijah could be in Fort Severn that long.

"What do you think about that, Elijah?" Ezra asked.

A faint twinkle appeared in Elijah's eyes as he lowered his tea cup. "You won't have to coax me," he replied. "I would like that very much. I am hungry for roast goose."

Silence reigned for a few minutes while breakfast was finished. Then Ezra turned to Lazarus while slowly nodding his head. "Yes, Lazarus, I agree with Elijah. Thank you for the invitation. Where will we go to hunt?"

Lazarus pushed out his lips and nodded his head toward the east. "Down past Partridge Island, near Hudson Bay, are large grassy flats along the river. At this time of the year, thousands of geese stop there to feed as they migrate south."

The first light of Tuesday morning found the three men situated on a grassy flat a few miles downriver from the Fort Severn settlement. The raw easterly wind pushed patches of mist and rain across the sky. Ezra was glad for his warm coat and equally happy to be sharing this special time with Christian friends. It was enjoyable to watch the brothers relate to each other as they waited for geese to appear. Lazarus was pretty good with the goose call, and soon a flock turned and headed in their direction. At Lazarus' signal, the men rose up and started shooting. Several geese fell heavily to the earth.

"Good shooting, Lazarus," exclaimed Elijah. "How many did you drop? Two?"

Lazarus nodded. "You also got one?"

"Yes," Elijah said. "It was my third shot, but at least I connected."

"Both of you are pretty good shots," Ezra chimed in. A rueful expression came over his face. "It seems there is a lot of open sky around those geese. Lazarus, are you sure there are BBs in my shells?"

The men enjoyed the morning hunt and motored back upstream to Fort Severn with their harvest. A nice collection of snow geese and a few Canada geese lay piled in the canoe. The afternoon was spent dressing the geese.

Wednesday morning was even better, with more Canada geese falling to their guns than the day before. After the hunt, the men once again headed back up river. About six miles of delta lay between the Hudson Bay and the settlement of Fort Severn. As the men started their journey, the outboard motor sputtered to a stop. Try as they might, it would not start. The river was too swift to make much headway by paddling. So they resorted to a method often used by Elijah and Lazarus' forefathers.

A rope was tied to the canoe, and Ezra and Elijah walked along the shore pulling the craft upriver. Lazarus sat in the canoe, skillfully keeping the canoe away from rocks and the river bank. They came to a branch in the river and the current was not as swift, so they all climbed in and succeeded in paddling across to the far shore of the branch. Then they had to tow the canoe with a rope again. It was hard work.

When they came within sight of the settlement, some people spotted them pulling their canoe. How grateful the men were to be discovered and even more grateful to see a motor boat heading their way across the river to pull them back to the village.

Thursday morning, Ezra and Elijah prepared to go home. While Elijah loaded the geese, Ezra refueled the airplane. He filled one tank completely and left the other about three gallons short of being topped off.

That should be plenty to get back to Bearskin, Ezra thought.

Besides, this plane is going to be heavy enough with two men and our geese. Ezra was taking three geese, and Elijah was taking sixteen. Elijah was not restricted to bag limits as Ezra was.

When the preflight inspection of the aircraft was completed, Ezra and Elijah climbed in and Ezra taxied out to take off. As he opened the throttle, Ezra knew without a doubt that he was heavily loaded. He worked hard to bring the plane up on step. After several attempts, he was able to lift one float above the water. This greatly reduced the drag, and the airspeed slowly increased. With a skillful maneuver, he lifted the other float from the river and they were airborne, heading down-river toward the Hudson Bay. When he gained an altitude of 800 feet, he gently banked and came around, heading back up past Fort Severn.

Shortly after becoming airborne, Ezra sensed that something did not seem quite right with the plane and decided to check the magnetos[1] once again as he had done before takeoff. When he switched to the right magneto, the engine had an obvious miss. Switching to the left magneto, the engine ran well. Something was wrong with the right magneto. Ezra selected the "both" position and continued on.

It would be quickest to head directly for Bearskin, Ezra thought, *but then I will have that thirty-mile dry hop with no lakes. I think I'll choose a little longer route that will keep me over water in case the engine acts up and I need to land.* Ezra also suspected that the combination of moisture and cold air temperature was icing up

---

[1] Magnetos are electric generators that use magnets to produce pulsing current for the ignition system in some engines.

the carburetor, causing the engine to run rich. He pulled the carburetor heat knob to alleviate the problem.

"Well, Elijah," announced Ezra some time later. He raised his voice to be heard over the engine noise. "I don't think we have enough gas to make it into Bearskin. There is a lake under us, and it looks suitable to land. The river up ahead has a lot of rocks, and I don't want to have to put down there. So here goes." Ezra banked the PA-12, lined up with where he wanted to land, and soon settled the airplane onto the water. They taxied to shore and climbed out.

"I first want to check the gas in the tanks," Ezra told Elijah. To his dismay, the one tank was completely empty, and only one inch of fuel remained in the other tank.

"It looks like we'll be camping here for the night," Ezra declared.

"We won't starve," Elijah answered. "We've got a plane load of geese."

The men set to securing the plane on the shore and taking stock of their situation.

"We have some emergency food in the back of the plane," remembered Ezra. "I also have the gizzards we saved when we cleaned the geese."

"I've got an idea about how to keep these geese from spoiling," added Elijah. "See this deep moss here? Watch this." He got down on his hands and knees and began pulling up large chunks of the moss growing on the ground. Soon he motioned for Ezra to join him. "Feel this," Elijah urged. "Put your hand down here below where the moss was. It is cold like a refrigerator." When the geese were all stored in the "fridge," he asked, "Where do you want to sleep?"

"I don't know," Ezra answered. "Where do you want to sleep?"

"I guess on the ground," Elijah replied.

They laid some extra clothes on the ground and then spread the Woods 5 Star sleeping bag over them. It was a top-of-the-line bag commonly carried as emergency gear in bush planes. An extra blanket served as their top cover. It wasn't like their beds at home, but the men slept as good as could be expected that night.

The next morning Elijah decided to roast a goose. He spent a good deal of time with the fire, preparing a bed of coals. He also fashioned a make-shift rotisserie with which to rotate the

^ Roast goose was Ezra and Elijah's main fare for several days as they waited for help to arrive.

goose above the hot coals. When all was ready, one of the geese was skewered onto a sharpened stick, and the cook was ready to proceed with roasting the goose.

Ezra watched, fascinated by Elijah's skill and the improvised set-up. The goose was roasting nicely and the tantalizing aroma was whetting his already keen appetite. "It looks to me like you have done this before," he said admiringly. "The sight and smell of that goose is making my mouth water."

Elijah smiled. "I remember saying on Monday that I was hungry for roasted goose, but I sure didn't expect it to happen this way."

When the goose was roasted, they removed it from the stick and cut it in half. Each man had half a goose for his meal. Before they ate, they bowed their heads.

"Thank you, heavenly Father, for your kind mercies to us," Ezra began. "Thank you again for bringing us safely to this spot and for your protection through the night. Thank you for this food and that Elijah knows how to prepare it so well. And Father, we seek your will in getting out of this place. When we are missed, help the searchers know where to look for us. Give us wisdom, we pray, that we may know what we ought to do here. Be with Nannie and Emma as they already may be wondering where we are. We ask these things in Jesus' name. Amen."

"Amen," joined in Elijah.

When Ezra and Elijah did not return home, concerned people in both Bearskin Lake and Red Lake made calls to find out what was happening. But radio signals were very poor on both Friday and Saturday, and the calls did not go through. Nannie also called Whitey Hostetler and Irwin Schantz, hoping to find out something about her husband's absence.

Nannie tried not to let her imagination run wild. *I am so grateful*

Ezra promised me when he began flying that he would not take chances with the airplane, she comforted herself. *Maybe they ran into bad weather and landed somewhere, waiting for better conditions.* She determined by the grace of God to trust Him for Ezra's protection and her family's future.

Nannie was finally able to get through to a radio operator on Tuesday. She informed him of Ezra's travel plans and let him know that the men were missing. The operator called around and discovered the men had left Fort Severn on Thursday but had not arrived at Bearskin. At last there was some direction as to where to start looking.

When Nannie heard those details, she considered a number of possibilities in her mind. *Perhaps they ran out of gas, landed, and were simply waiting for help to arrive. Maybe something unexpected happened and the plane crashed. Is Ezra alive? Is he injured? Could it be that he died?* Determined not to allow her emotions to get the best of her and make her think the worst, she turned again to the Lord, pouring out her burden to Him.

Meanwhile, Ezra and Elijah were making the best of their unexpected camping trip. Elijah retrieved another goose from under the moss and prepared another tasty meal. Both Thursday and Friday nights were spent on the ground sharing the sleeping bag and blanket. Saturday afternoon, however, the sky began to darken.

"I think it might rain tonight," Elijah ventured. "What do you want to do?"

"What do you want to do, Elijah?" returned Ezra.

"I think we should make a little shelter to keep us out of the rain," Elijah answered.

"Well, you are the *ogimaa*, Elijah," said Ezra. "You give the orders, and I'll help."

First the men placed a pole horizontally between two trees. Elijah cut saplings and laid the thick end of each one on the horizontal pole and the thin end on the ground below. Ezra's job was to cut pine branches to place on the saplings to keep the rain off.

Unfortunately, Elijah and Ezra had not laid down the branches quite right, so the roof leaked badly that night. The next morning they removed the pine boughs and re-laid them, starting at ground level and working up the sloped saplings. Then the pine branches worked more like shingles and shed the rain better.

"Well, Ezra," Elijah announced Sunday morning. "I think we should try to find some other food to eat."

"Why is that?" Ezra wanted to know. "Surely we have not eaten all the geese."

"I don't know how long it will be until these geese start to spoil," Elijah answered. "I see there are signs of rabbits in the area, and I have snare wire with me. I am going to try to snare some rabbits to eat."

On Monday afternoon the wind picked up and the sky grew ominously dark. Before long it began to rain heavily. It rained and rained and rained. The wind grew stronger by the hour.

"I'm going to try to tie the plane down more securely," Ezra said. "With this wind, I am concerned it might blow the plane into the trees on the shore."

Together the men used what rope they had and fastened the plane the best they could. Still the wind kept increasing.

"What do you think we should do, Ezra?" Elijah asked.

"Let's get in the airplane," Ezra answered. "That sheds rain far better than our shelter. Also, our weight will help keep the plane from being blown away." A few minutes later the wet men were inside the fuselage while the wind lashed rain against the fabric of the plane. Before long, the windows were steamed up and they could see little outside. All of a sudden, Ezra blurted, "Look at that!"

"What?" the startled Elijah inquired.

"Look at the air speed indicator," Ezra exclaimed. "It is registering between 30 and 40! That is not far below takeoff speed."

Again the men turned to their heavenly Father and committed their care into His hands. It was a long and tense night; only after the worst of the storm had passed could the men rest.

※ ※ ※ ※ ※ ※ ※ ※ ※ ※ ※ ※ ※ ※ ※ ※ ※ ※ ※ ※

"Morning, Paul," drawled Whitey Hostetler. "I suppose you heard by now that Ezra didn't get back from Fort Severn last week."

Paul Fry knew Whitey well enough to read the concern in the tone of his voice. "Yes, I did hear that."

"Well, Nannie got word this morning that Ezra and Elijah left the Fort last Thursday but never got to Bearkskin," Whitey said. "I'm thinking we ought to get on the move and have a look. Would you be available to go along? Two pairs of eyes are better than one."

"Sure, I'm available," Paul said immediately. "When do we go?"

"Well, Irwin Schantz said we could use MIC's 180, and they are gassing it up right now. Weather doesn't look the best, but

I really think we should get off as soon as possible. Can you be ready in twenty minutes?"

"I'll be ready and waiting for you at the mission dock," Paul answered.

It was not a pleasant day for flying. Gusty winds and lowering clouds made flying a challenge. Whitey was at the controls as the Cessna neared Muskrat Dam. By now the thick cloud cover had pushed them closer to the ground and made navigation difficult. They had to skirt around some areas where the clouds were down to the trees. Whitey glanced over at his companion. Paul Fry was also a pilot for NLGM, and he had spent considerable time flying this Cessna. Whitey knew Paul was not a reckless pilot.

"Shall we go on?" Whitey asked.

"I would have turned back long ago," Paul replied.

"Look!" Whitey peered forward. "It looks like conditions are a little better ahead. Let's press on for a bit and see whether that continues."

A few minutes later they passed the Muskrat Dam Settlement and visibility improved slightly. Both men were able to relax a bit as the weather improved. Before long they landed at Bearskin Lake to refuel. They also inquired whether there was any more news concerning the whereabouts of Ezra and Elijah. There was none.

Meanwhile, back at Red Lake, a knock sounded on the Peacheys' door.

"Well, hello, Esther," greeted Nannie. "Please come in."

"Good morning, Nannie," Esther Hostetler began as she entered and set a box on the kitchen table. "Our thoughts and prayers are with you in all the uncertainty you are facing right now."

"Thank you so much for your care and concern," Nannie answered. "I heard that your husband and Paul left to look for Ezra and Elijah."

"Yes, they did," acknowledged Esther. "I am glad that radio signals are better today. That way we can at least be kept informed about what is going on."

Nannie did not say anything and Esther continued.

"I brought an extra radio receiver that is on the same frequency used by NLGM and their aircraft. I thought you might like to use it to keep up with what is happening on the search," she offered.

Nannie looked at the radio and back to Esther. Then Nannie gazed thoughtfully at nothing in particular. After a few moments she replied. "That is so thoughtful of you to bring this over here for me. But . . ." She paused some long moments. "But I'm not sure listening would be helpful for me. It . . . it might make me more tense. I am trying to trust God instead of dwelling on worrying thoughts. I would rather wait until they know what happened. Does that make sense to you, Esther?"

"Yes, I think I understand," Esther replied. "God bless you and keep you in His care while you wait."

※ ※ ※ ※ ※ ※ ※ ※ ※ ※ ※ ※ ※ ※ ※ ※ ※ ※ ※ ※

Tuesday, back at the campsite, Ezra and Elijah were concerned. They knew their wives would be worried by now. How they wished the plane had a radio. The only device they had was an Emergency Locator Transmitter (ELT). Ezra told Elijah how it worked.

"Some of these ELTs activate automatically when an airplane crashes," he explained. "Others, like this one, need to be activated. You've probably wondered why I keep carrying this thing around inside my jacket. I want to keep the battery warm, because a warm battery will have more power to transmit the emergency signal. I have been turning it on whenever the weather is good enough for flying. Hopefully, the searchers will pick up the signal and be able to locate us."

"That makes sense," Elijah responded. "We've also got a good fire going, and I have a nice pile of pine branches ready. When we hear a plane, we will pile these green branches on the fire to make lots of smoke."

Tuesday afternoon Elijah suddenly exclaimed, "I hear a plane!"

The men scrambled to pile the green pine boughs on the fire. They soon saw the airplane come out over the lake where they were stranded, heading for Fort Severn. How they prayed their signal would be heard and their smoke seen!

Whitey and Paul had taken off from Bearskin and gained sufficient altitude to be able to see a good distance to the left and right. Both men were intensely scanning the terrain and shorelines below for a glimpse of an airplane.

"There's an ELT signal!" exclaimed Whitey. "Mark our location on the map where we picked up the signal. We'll keep going and see whether the signal gets stronger or weaker."

Within minutes the signal strength weakened, so Whitey banked the plane around to the east. The ELT signal soon became stronger again.

"Look!" Paul cried. "There's a plane on the far shore."

"Got it," answered Whitey. Both men peered intently through the windshield as they flew closer. "And isn't that two men by a campfire?" Whitey asked. "Let's try to determine more before we make a call."

As they passed over Ezra and Elijah, the pilots were gratified to see the plane was not wrecked and the men appeared active and well. Whitey applied full throttle and pulled the 180 into a steep climb. Higher altitude meant better radio transmission and reception. He banked the plane to circle the lake while he keyed the mike.

"BYA to CJR-351, BYA to CJR-351," he repeated.

"CJR-351 to BYA, over," the reply came.

"We have found the men," Whitey began. "Their plane is parked on a lake and the men are beside their campfire. All appear okay from up here. We will know more when we land and speak with them. Over."

"Praise the Lord! Thank you for the report. We will let Nannie know. Over and out."

※※※※※※※※※※※※※※※※※※※※

At their house on Skookum Bay, Nannie wondered when word would come concerning the fate of her husband and Elijah. And when the word did come, what would it be? She was fully aware of the possibility that something serious had happened. The Peacheys' fourteen-year-old, Nathaniel, was also trying to process thoughts of what his future might hold if his father had died in an accident.

Rrrrrring. With a sense of anticipation and trepidation, Nannie stepped over to the telephone. "Hello."

"Hello, Nannie," a familiar voice said. "This is Irwin calling, and I have good news for you!"

A deep sense of relief washed over Nannie. "What is it?" She could barely speak.

"Whitey and Paul have found Ezra and Elijah on a lake not far from Bearskin. From the air they saw the plane parked by the shore and the men standing by their campfire waving at them. The airplane is not wrecked, and the men appear well."

"Praise the Lord," was all Nannie could say.

"We will let you know more details later when we find out what happened. Whitey is landing now, and more details should be forthcoming when they are airborne again. Susan and I are so happy for you, Nannie, and we are grateful to God for this outcome. God bless you!"

Having radioed Red Lake with their initial assessment, Whitey scanned the lake below for wind direction and possible rocks in the water. After descending downwind, he circled to the right to line up his approach into the wind. Almost by instinct, he lowered the flaps and adjusted the throttle accordingly. As the Cessna settled lower, both men were observing the lake conditions. They could read the gusts of wind that ruffled and darkened the surface of the lake and momentarily lifted the plane as it passed through them. In a few more moments, Whitey gently pulled back the yoke to position the plane in the correct attitude for landing. Just as the stall warning buzzer sounded, the floats connected with the lake surface with a rapid staccato of bumps. Gradually the plane's momentum was lost, and they were gently floating on the water.

Whitey lowered the water rudders and turned to Paul. "I wonder what we will find," he said, half-questioningly.

Paul answered, "I guess we will soon find out. If it is something as simple as needing more gas, we will be able to help them. Thank God they are alive, and the plane is not wrecked."

In a few more minutes, Whitey switched off the ignition and guided the drifting plane to shore. Ezra and Elijah were waiting to catch the plane, and broad smiles wreathed their faces.

"Are we ever glad to see you!" Ezra called out to Paul, who was standing on the right pontoon.

"We are grateful to God to see you two alive and well!" replied Paul.

It didn't take long to find out the reason the men had been forced down on this lonely lake. Ezra explained why he thought they had run low on fuel. "After we got airborne at Fort Severn," Ezra said, "the right magneto began to miss, and that meant the fuel wasn't being burned efficiently. Also, since the carburetor kept icing up, I had to fly with the carb heat on, which also burned more fuel. Besides all that, I realized partway here that we were flying into an unexpectedly strong headwind."

Both pilots nodded their heads in understanding.

"We brought some gas along," Whitey said. Paul was already preparing to strain the gas through a chamois into the wing tank.

"Whitey," asked Ezra, "would you be willing to fly this plane into Bearskin? You know airplanes and engines better than I do, and I am a little nervous about that right mag not working properly."

"No problem," Whitey answered. "Paul can fly the Cessna to Bearskin. I'll check out the PA-12."

While the three pilots were discussing those options, Elijah was on his knees retrieving the remaining geese. He smelled them and pronounced them still fit to eat, so the men loaded them into the Cessna for the short flight to Bearskin.

By the time they got to Bearskin, Whitey had confirmed that something was indeed wrong with the right magneto. He unbolted it from the PA-12 and flew it with him in the Cessna over to a mechanic shop on Big Trout Lake.

Back in Bearskin, Elijah was very grateful to be reunited with Emma. Ezra and Paul spent the night in Bearskin as well. As Ezra drifted off to sleep in a more comfortable bed, he breathed a prayer of thankfulness to God. It was a relief to finally be rescued.

When Whitey returned the next morning, he reported that the cause of the problem had been found. A gasket had leaked and allowed oil to get into the magneto, thus shorting it out. The repaired magneto was soon bolted back in the PA-12, and Whitey flew it back to Red Lake.

Paul and Ezra flew home in the Cessna. Paul had many questions, and Ezra had several hours to recount the events of the past week. Apart from missing Nannie and their three sons, Ezra had enjoyed the days in the wild with Elijah. He marveled at Elijah's knowledge and expertise at "roughing it." Ezra would later draw illustrations for his teaching from the lessons he had learned.

It had truly been an unexpected camping trip.

18

A VISIT TO THE BUNKHOUSE

"What are you planning to do this afternoon?" Nannie asked her husband as they ate lunch one Sunday.

"I thought of going over to the forestry bunkhouse to visit Jimmy Keesic," Ezra replied. "Since it has been raining off and on the past week, he will likely have some time to talk. He usually has things he wants to talk about."

After the meal, Ezra pushed back from the table and glanced outside to check on the weather. It was raining again.

"Thanks for the tasty lunch, dear," he said as he pulled on his raincoat and headed for the door. "It will probably be a couple hours until I return."

"God bless you, dear," smiled Nannie. "May God give you wisdom in what you talk about. I'm glad you can be an encouragement to Jimmy, especially since he has given his heart to the Lord."

A short time later Jimmy welcomed Ezra into the bunkhouse for a visit. Their conversations were often on varied subjects, and today was no exception.

"How is your work as a firefighting officer going?" Ezra asked as they sat in Jimmy's room.

"This fire season has been a busy one," Jimmy replied. "The fire southwest of Red Lake was huge. We brought in a lot of men from the reserves to help fight that fire. The rain we got over the past week really helped us mop up the hot spots. Right now we are waiting to see what might develop next."

"What exactly do you do?" Ezra wondered.

"I notify the men on the reserves when we need firefighters," Jimmy answered. "When they come to the forestry station here, I help them understand what their duties will be. I also show them where they will eat and sleep when they stay here. It really helps that I can speak both English and the native language."

"Do you like what you are doing?" Ezra inquired.

"I am very happy with my job. I enjoy working on the forestry staff with the fire fighters. I really like my work," Jimmy replied.

"That's a good thing," Ezra acknowledged. "Ecclesiastes says 'there is nothing better for a man, than that he should eat and drink, and that he should make his soul enjoy good in his labor.' "

Jimmy nodded his head.

"We missed you at church this morning," Ezra said. "I've forgotten what your schedule is like over the firefighting season."

"I am the weekend officer every three weeks," Jimmy explained. "I'm required to stay here to organize things if a fire situation should develop. With the rain these last couple days, I don't expect to get a call today, but I have to remain on duty."

"I can understand that," Ezra replied. "I wanted you to know that we missed you this morning. We always look forward to seeing you in church. In fact, would it suit you to lead singing again next Sunday?"

"You want me to lead singing again after all the mistakes I made the last time?" Jimmy sounded surprised.

"What mistakes?" Ezra questioned.

"Well, like forgetting to sing the last verse of one song, and starting another on too high a pitch. It's sort of embarrassing."

"Yes, I remember now," Ezra admitted. "But most everyone I know who has led singing makes those mistakes. A wise song leader learns from his errors and tries to do better the next time. I believe you are learning well; at least, to me it seems you are making fewer mistakes the longer you have led singing. I hope you don't give up."

"Oh, I'm not giving up," Jimmy stated. "And I'm willing to try again next week."

"Thank you," said Ezra. "God bless you for being willing to serve the congregation."

"Changing the subject, there is something I wanted to ask you about." Jimmy shifted in his chair. He noted Ezra's attentive expression and continued. "Remember a month or so ago when that healing preacher came to Red Lake and held those tent meetings?"

Ezra nodded his head.

"I know you and Nannie don't agree with some of those things, but I wanted to see what was happening there," Jimmy admitted. "So I went one evening when I was off duty."

"What did you find?" Ezra wanted to know.

"People were falling down when the preacher prayed for them," Jimmy answered. "They called it something like . . . being slain, yes, being slain in the spirit. That's what they called it. I wanted to know what this was all about. The preacher invited anyone who desired to come up, and he would pray for them. So I went forward."

Ezra was intently watching and listening as his young friend related his experience.

"He prayed for me," Jimmy went on, "but I didn't fall down. I was tempted to fake it, though. And the next day, some of my friends told me that I must not be a Christian because I didn't fall down. One suggested I might not even be saved. That kind of troubled me. So that is what I wanted to ask you about."

"What is it you wanted to know?" Ezra probed.

"About that thing of being slain in the spirit," Jimmy replied. "Is that right or wrong? I remember in Bible school you often taught something about the spirits of the prophets being subject to prophets. I have been wondering whether being slain in the spirit is connected to those verses."

"I believe it is, Jimmy," Ezra began. "But allow me to explain a few things that we believe the Bible teaches. When Jesus told His disciples about the Holy Spirit's coming, He pointed out some important things by which we will recognize that it is the Holy Spirit of God. Jesus said that when the Spirit of truth is come, He will guide us into all truth. So the Holy Spirit will always be true to the Word of God. Jesus also said that the Holy Spirit will not speak of Himself, but will speak what He hears, and He will show us things to come. The Holy Spirit will glorify Jesus, for He will take what He hears from Jesus and will reveal it to man.

"So we understand that the Holy Spirit doesn't draw attention to Himself, but to Jesus Christ. The Holy Spirit isn't going about trying to exalt Himself, but rather to turn men's hearts to obey the Lord. Jimmy, when these things were going on up front, was your heart being drawn to glorify the preacher, the Holy Spirit, or Jesus Christ?"

"I'd have to think about that," Jimmy replied, still pondering. "He spoke a lot about being filled with and getting the gifts of the Spirit. The preacher taught that when he prays for you and you are filled, then you will be slain in the spirit and will speak in tongues. He claimed that when he prays for sick people, they are healed."

Ezra explained further. "The Bible says very clearly that the Holy Spirit gives differing gifts and abilities to every man as HE wills. The gifts and manifestations of the Holy Spirit are not about exalting a man or about making him appear more spiritual than the next person. The Holy Spirit is truly about building the church, and He does not contradict God's Word. When the Holy Spirit of God fills your mind, Jimmy, you will not lose your mind and become senseless, or laugh uncontrollably, or bark like a dog. A spirit is definitely working in those things you observed, but we do not believe it is the Holy Spirit of God. The Holy Spirit does not take over your mind; rather, when God's Spirit speaks to you, then you should voluntarily yield to Him. You will know what the Holy Spirit is speaking to your mind and heart."

"That makes a lot of sense," Jimmy answered, "but it can be pretty confusing when so many people get so excited about being slain. If I understand you right, people will get excited about obeying the Word of God if it's the Holy Spirit at work. Is that right?"

"That is right, my friend!" Ezra exclaimed. "The things you saw may produce exciting and dramatic experiences, but Jesus is concerned that we live out His Word in everyday life. The Holy Spirit has been sent to encourage and help us to do that."

"This discussion has been helpful," Jimmy said. "Thank you for taking the time to explain these things to me. By the way, I've got some cookies and juice here. Would you like some?"

"I would, Jimmy," Ezra answered. "Thank you for your kindness."

As Jimmy placed the snacks on the table, he said, "There's one other thing I wanted to talk to you about. It has to do with what you taught us about money when I went to the Red Lake Indian School."

"What are you thinking about?" Ezra inquired.

"Oh, about how you told us to save some money from each paycheck," Jimmy explained. "Then when I need something, I can purchase it with cash instead of charging it and paying interest."

"Is that what you are doing?" Ezra wanted to know.

"Yes I am!" Jimmy declared. "That was a big thing for me. Up until the time you taught us that, I used to really admire people who could go to the store and charge whatever they wanted. When I saw somebody who could buy an expensive item and charge it, I would say, 'Wow!' I wanted to be like that.

"But now I have learned how helpful it is to save money until I have enough to buy what I need. It also has made me more careful about what I decide to buy. Right now I am saving to get a vehicle. If all goes well, by the end of the summer I should have enough for a decent used car. Then I can get around better without having to find a ride with someone else."

"That certainly is commendable," Ezra acknowledged. "When

you buy a car, though, it will bring other tests into your life."

"What do you mean by that?" Jimmy questioned.

"When some young men buy cars," Ezra told him, "they discover many places they want to go. Sometimes they don't seem to have time to come to church and worship God anymore. I hope that doesn't happen to you."

"I don't plan on that happening," Jimmy replied. "I want to use my time and money in a way that pleases God. Every couple weeks I am reminded of how easy it is to waste a paycheck."

"How is that?" Ezra asked.

"When a man comes in from the bush after fighting a fire for many days, he gets a pretty big pay check," Jimmy explained. "Instead of saving some and spending the rest wisely, he may spend his whole check on booze and a week later have nothing to show for all his hard work. I really wonder how a man can keep going that way. It's not a wise way to live."

"You are right, and I'm glad that you understand these things, Jimmy," Ezra said. "Many of your people and mine live their whole lives spending their money as fast or faster than they earn it. God shows us a better way in His Word."

"Thank you again, Ezra, for teaching me these things. I believe I am a better man for it. Pray for me that I will keep God's ways before my eyes. I want to live simply and glorify God as I see you and Nannie doing," Jimmy confessed.

Ezra got up and reached for his coat. "Thank you for your kind words, my friend. I think I will try to take a short nap before supper and the evening service. May we pray before I go?"

Both men bowed their heads and lifted grateful voices to their heavenly Father for the time spent together, for being able to hold and read God's Word, and for Jesus Christ who lived within. They prayed for the salvation of friends who did not yet know the Lord.

In later years, Jimmy recalled his many visits with Ezra and how they usually ended in prayer. "That is how I learned to pray out loud," Jimmy said. "Ezra told me I don't have to use fancy words when I pray. All I had to do was tell God in my own words what is on my heart. Ezra told me I can be honest with God and tell Him exactly how I feel. I am grateful to Ezra for teaching me these things about prayer."

19
CHURCH BUILDING AT BEARSKIN

Ezra was enjoying this flight. MIC had recently purchased its own Cessna 180 from a local man in Red Lake, and Ezra had diligently trained himself to fly it safely. The feel of the Cessna 180's controls had become familiar to him by this time, and he was more relaxed as he flew along. A July morning sun was shining through the thin veil of clouds and warming the landscape below him. Ezra had trimmed the plane to crab into the steady northwest breeze to keep him on his flight path. MacDowell Lake had slipped beneath the left wing awhile back, and soon Weagamow Lake would be visible off to the right. Then he would intersect the mighty, muddy Severn River, east of where it received an influx of clean water as it passed Muskrat Dam. It always amazed Ezra how quickly that clean water lost its clarity when combined with the dirty Severn. From there on, if a pilot wanted to, he could simply follow the river below to Bearskin Lake.

Ezra anticipated meeting Elijah and David and the small band of Christ's disciples at Bearskin. *What was it they had said? Something about a church building?*

^ The first Bearskin Lake Mennonite Church building, reconstructed from a salvaged log building.

Upon landing, Ezra was met by Elijah and David and a number of other people who gathered around. When the floatplane had been securely tied and the excitement of his arrival had worn off, Ezra was invited to Elijah's house for something to eat. There Ezra learned of the project already underway.

The believers in Bearskin had wanted a church house in which to meet. Funds for building were limited, so the men had explored other options. An old log building on the other side of the lake had sat in disuse for some years. The men received permission to take it down and use the logs for their church. The structure was torn down log by log and brought to where the new church would be built. Then, in reverse order, the building was reconstructed. It measured about twenty feet by twenty-eight feet.

CHURCH BUILDING AT BEARSKIN

Ezra was amazed at what had already been accomplished. With few resources other than willing hearts and hands, the project was moving along rapidly. A lot of help was coming from the community. Such practical support was evidence of the growing goodwill toward the Christians.

◆◆◆◆◆◆◆◆◆◆◆◆◆◆◆◆◆◆◆◆◆◆◆

The church house was completed in approximately one month. Someone made a donation to the project, and Ezra used the money to purchase an insulated chimney in Red Lake, which he then flew to Bearskin. Ezra joined the men for a day or two to help erect the building, but the project was initiated and completed

∧ A framed church house replaced the original log structure.

by the local people in Bearskin. They put up a sign, written in both English and the local language, that read: Bearskin Lake Mennonite Church. Several years later, the church people built a framed church house to replace the original log structure.

20
A SERVANT FALLS

A deep groan emerged from Ezra's throat as he read the words before him. He pulled a handkerchief from his pocket and wiped at the tears that began trickling down his cheeks.

"What's the matter, dear?" Nannie came over and stood beside her husband. "What is going on?"

Ezra slowly shook his head, unable to speak at the moment. He handed the letter to his wife. She took it and looked first to see who had written.

"It's from Greta," she noted under her breath. Silence reigned as Nannie read the words on the page before her.

Ezra lifted his eyes to watch his wife. He observed the shadow of grief that washed over her countenance as her eyes traced back and forth. She finished reading and handed the letter back to Ezra. She stood in silence as both of them tried to digest the shocking news. After some minutes, Ezra spoke.

"The Apostle John wrote, 'I have no greater joy than to hear that my children walk in truth,' " he began, "and I wonder whether there is any greater sorrow than to hear that my spiritual children walk in sin." He paused awhile before continuing. "What has this done to the cause of Christ and David's testimony in the community? Proverbs says that 'whoso committeth adultery with a woman lacketh understanding: he that doeth it destroyeth his own soul. A wound and dishonor shall he get, and his reproach shall not be wiped away.' "

"I was thinking of what Greta must be going through," Nannie said. "Such unfaithfulness strikes at the very heart of the sacred union of man and wife."

"Yes, it does," agreed Ezra. "From what she writes, though, it seems she believes he is sorry. My first concern is along those same lines. Is he truly repentant?"

"I hope and pray that Greta has forgiven her husband," Nannie added. "That must be one of the hardest things a wife can face in her entire life."

Neither said anything for a few minutes. Then Ezra spoke up. "Let's pray about this."

Together Ezra and Nannie knelt and poured out their hearts to God. They prayed that David's repentance would indeed be sincere, and that his life would reflect that repentance. Ezra prayed that God would continue to build the church at Bearskin in spite of this tragic incident. Nannie interceded fervently for Greta, that Greta would live in forgiveness toward David and that trust might be restored in their marriage. As they concluded their prayer, Ezra asked God for wisdom in understanding the situation and for direction in how to proceed.

Shortly afterward, Ezra flew to Bearskin Lake. It was a somber

David who recognized Ezra's plane and came to meet him at the dock. He invited Ezra to his house. Very little was said as each man sipped his cup of strong tea. Long minutes of silence were not unusual in that culture, and Ezra prayed silently that he might know how to proceed. Finally he spoke.

"We read your wife's letter," Ezra began quietly.

David nodded almost imperceptibly, his downcast eyes staring at the table.

"We were so saddened to read what Greta wrote about your adultery," Ezra continued. "Is it true, David?"

David shifted uncomfortably on his chair and glanced up briefly. "Yes, that is true, Ezra."

Ezra was silent for a few minutes, trying to find the right words to properly frame his next question. "What are you thinking now about what you have done?" he asked.

"I am so ashamed to have sinned like that. It was wrong," David stated.

Ezra was silent and waited.

"I have sinned against God and my wife," David continued. "After all Jesus has done to save me and help me through these years, there is no excuse for doing what I did. Already people are saying bad things about me and the church."

"What are they saying?" Ezra wondered.

"Some think I should not be working in the church anymore," David said.

Ezra nodded his head understandingly and again silently waited for David to continue.

"A few people said they don't want anything to do with

Christianity if that is how Christians act." David paused as if searching for more words. "And I am afraid I have given them good reason to say such things."

"Why do you say that, David?" Ezra questioned.

"At first I tried to deny that anything had happened between me and her," David confessed. "But it became obvious after a while that she was expecting a baby. When the baby came, she claimed it was my child. That was when I admitted I was the baby's father. I am so sorry."

"What are you sorry for?" Ezra probed.

"I don't really understand what you mean by that question. I am sorry for sinning against God and committing adultery!" David exclaimed. "Don't you believe me, Ezra?"

"Yes, David," Ezra said gently, "I believe you are sorry. I asked that question because I need to know whether you are truly sorry for your sin, or if you are only sorry because your sin has been discovered and now people are saying things. Do you understand the difference?"

There was silence for a few minutes as David considered Ezra's question. "I think I understand," he said simply.

"Maybe I should explain a bit further," Ezra offered. "If you had come forward and owned up to it when you realized you had sinned, people might more easily conclude that you were truly sorry. But when you denied being involved with her and only admitted your sin after she claimed the baby was yours, then it raises the question whether you are only sorry because you have been caught. Does that make sense?"

David nodded his head. "Yes, it does. I should have confessed it right away. The way this came out has been hard on my family and the church. I am so sorry for the grief I caused them."

"Thank you for speaking so openly with me, David," Ezra responded. "I believe your repentance is sincere, and I want you to know I forgive you. I also need to admonish you to live in humility and brokenness as people say things about this from time to time. The sincerity of your repentance will be evident by how well you accept the reaping that comes from sowing this sin. Remember what King David reaped for his sin with Bathsheba in the Bible? Even though God assured David that his sin was forgiven, David experienced life-long consequences. Never once do we read of David complaining about the severity of those things."

"I have already experienced some of what you are talking about," David replied. "Some people don't trust or respect me like they did before this happened, and I know those things will need to be earned again.

"Besides that," David continued, "the woman's husband was angry with me and had some hard things to say. I listened to him and told him what I did was wrong and that I am sorry. I asked him if there is anything more I can do to make it right. You will never guess what he asked of me."

"What was that?" Ezra inquired.

"He asked me to give him my snowmobile. It was a nice machine that I used for trapping and getting around in the winter. It cost me a lot of money, but when he asked me for it, I gave it to him. It seems that straightened things out with him. At least he is friendlier to me since then," David concluded.

"You acted wisely in granting his request," Ezra answered. "I am grateful to hear how you responded. I trust that will help convince him that you are sorry for what you did."

Later, Ezra met with the believers at the Bearskin church. He listened as some of the believers told how David's actions had affected their lives in the community. Ezra was happy to hear many expressions of forgiveness toward David and a desire to see him continue living in repentance and humility. Many expressed caution regarding David's future responsibilities as a leader in the church. Ever since Elijah and David had become Christians and moved home from Red Lake, they had shared the informal leadership role. Now, the believers made it clear to Ezra that they wanted only Elijah to be their church leader. After the meeting, several men thanked Ezra for coming to assist them.

When Ezra's Cessna 180 had climbed up from the lake and leveled off for his return flight to Red Lake, Ezra realized what a tremendous weight had lifted from his shoulders. As he flew, he worshipped the Lord and rejoiced in the way He had led in the work at Bearskin.

Ezra was convinced of David's repentance. He was eager to tell Nannie of how Greta accepted this difficult circumstance in her life and received God's grace to forgive her husband. Ezra believed the church had worked through their initial anger and betrayal and had come to a place of forgiveness in restoring David to the fellowship of the church. God had truly answered Ezra and Nannie's prayers.

21
INCIDENTS IN THE AIR

After Ezra began flying MIC's Cessna 180, it was necessary, in pilots' lingo, to be "checked out."[1] One day Whitey had some business in Redditt, a small community eighty-five miles south of Red Lake, near Kenora. Whitey and Ezra decided this was a good chance for Ezra to be checked out by Whitey.

The flight to Redditt was uneventful. While returning to Red Lake, however, Ezra noticed the fuel level in the right wing tank was not changing. "I wonder why the right tank is not going down like the left one," Ezra mentioned to Whitey. "Any ideas?"

"I suspect it is because you are flying with the one wing lower than the other," Whitey replied. "That is why the right tank is not draining properly."

Ezra wasn't so sure that was the case, but he didn't say anything. After all, he was the one being checked out. He thought about turning the fuel selector away from the "both" setting and

---

[1] To be observed and critiqued on an actual flight to evaluate a pilot's readiness to operate that aircraft safely.

selecting only the right tank. Before reaching for the selector, another thought came to mind. *If something is blocking the fuel flow from the right tank, switching only to that tank means the engine will lose power.* Ezra turned his gaze to the lake below and saw a lot of large snowdrifts covering the surface. *Not a good place to land in an emergency*, he thought. *I should wait for a lake with better landing conditions.*

Looking through the windshield and then confirming their position on the map lying on his lap, Ezra saw their route was taking them across a dry hop, a stretch of wilderness with no lakes. *I'm going to edge over toward Gullrock Lake,* Ezra reasoned silently. *I'd feel more comfortable if we were nearer a lake. There are more suitable landing choices available there if we run out of gas.*

They were halfway across the dry hop when the engine suddenly lost power. The left tank had been drained completely dry, and the gas would not feed from the right tank.

"I'll take the plane," Whitey said.

Ezra was happy to surrender the controls. Whitey skillfully used their altitude to glide the Cessna to a smooth dead-stick landing [2] in a sheltered bay on Gullrock Lake.

Ezra breathed a sigh of relief and looked gratefully over at Whitey. "Nice landing."

Whitey grunted his acknowledgment while he thought. "I guess we'll have to walk out to the road," Whitey said ruefully after a few moments.

---

[2] A no-power landing. This term originated in the days when airplanes had wooden propellers. If the plane would lose power, the propeller was nothing more than a "dead stick."

"I hope not," said Ezra as he crawled to the back of the plane's cabin. "I have a pump stored here that I prepared to transfer gas from barrels to the plane. I think it will work to transfer gas from the full tank to the empty one."

A few minutes later Ezra was manning the pump on the right wing tank, and Whitey was using a chamois to filter the gasoline as it flowed into the left wing tank. Ezra pumped until Whitey figured they had enough in the left tank to make it home. After Ezra drained and stowed the pump, they were ready to go, with Whitey flying the plane this time.

Once airborne, Whitey and Ezra had only about twenty miles to Red Lake. Whitey decided to follow the river in case they needed to land again. He turned the selector to the right tank, and immediately the engine began sputtering for lack of fuel. Quickly he turned it back to the left tank for the remainder of the trip.

When the airplane was warmed up in Whitey's hanger to check out the problem, gasoline flowed freely from the right tank. A small amount of frozen moisture in the fuel line was the cause of their worries that day. It was an inexpensive problem to fix.

Weather-wise, it had been a nice day for flying, and Ezra was relaxed as he landed the Cessna on the frozen surface of Bearskin Lake. He was returning from Fort Severn where he had spent a couple days visiting Lazarus and Modina Beardy. Here at Bearskin, Ezra was planning to gas up for the remainder of his trip home to Red Lake.

As Ezra taxied toward shore, he saw several people coming toward the plane. After he shut off the engine and climbed out onto the ice, he recognized several of the men. By the time of this visit, Ezra was well known at Bearskin, and the group that gathered upon his arrival was testimony to the community's good will toward him.

Several of the men who had come to greet him were hoping Ezra could fly them out a short distance and drop them off to hunt moose. But there was something else going on. As Ezra was considering the moose-hunting request, David Mosquito joined the group and made his way forward to greet his mentor.

After the usual greetings and inquiries, David got right to the point. "Elijah went out trapping a few days ago, and he was planning to be back by now. He has not returned. Do you think we could go look for him?"

"Yes, David, I think we should do that," Ezra answered. "Do you know where he went to trap?"

David nodded.

"Could you show me that area on my map?" Ezra asked.

"I can do that," David answered.

When Ezra saw the area pointed out on the map, he quickly calculated the amount of time it might take to find Elijah. "Are you ready to go along with me, David?" he asked. "We should probably go right away."

"I'm ready to go now," David answered. "I just hope everything is okay with Elijah."

Both men climbed into the 180, and soon they were in the air heading for Elijah's trapping area. They circled the area looking for fresh snowmobile tracks, but they found none.

"Do you know where his cabin is located?" Ezra yelled over the noise of the engine.

David nodded his head, and taking the map, he soon pointed to the place. A few minutes later Ezra dipped his left wing as he flew over the rustic building below. "I think he must be here," Ezra stated, "because there are fresh tracks in the snow around the cabin. Let me circle and take another look."

By the time Ezra had banked the airplane and come around for another pass, they could see Elijah standing outside, waving his hand to his visitors above. A few minutes later they taxied into the bay.

"Are you well?" Ezra asked as he and David climbed out.

"I'm fine," answered Elijah, "but my snowmobile isn't. The drive belt gave out, and I don't have an extra one."

"What do you want to do?" Ezra asked.

"I would like to go back to Bearskin with you," Elijah quickly answered.

"I'm happy to take you home, my friend," Ezra replied. "Are there things you need to do here before we go?"

"Not really. I just have to make sure the stove is okay, and I'll gather a few items. I will be ready before long," Elijah promised.

Twenty minutes later, Ezra touched down on Bearskin Lake for the second time that day. Again a group of men and children gathered around to see what was happening. Heads nodded in understanding when they heard of Elijah's trouble with his snowmobile. Many of them knew first-hand what it was like for equipment to fail.

The men who had asked earlier to be taken out to hunt now renewed their request. Ezra wanted to help the men, but he also was aware that doing so might jeopardize his chances of making it home yet that evening.

As Ezra gassed up his airplane, he made his decision. He would fly the hunters out. By the time he had finished refueling, the men were ready. They climbed in and Ezra took off, heading where the men wanted to go. A few minutes later Ezra felt a gentle tap on his right shoulder. One of the men asked whether they could fly over to another lake just to look around for signs of moose. "It's not far," the man said.

Ezra made a big circle where the man wanted to look, and no signs of moose were seen.

"There is another place we should look," they told Ezra. "It isn't much farther, over in that direction." The man pushed out his lips and nodded his head toward the east.

Ezra complied, wondering how long this might go on. By the time the men had decided where they wanted to hunt, Ezra knew he was running short on time to return to Red Lake. *I will just go as far as I safely can*, he thought. When he dropped the men off, he did not stop the engine. As soon as they were safely away from the airplane, Ezra opened the throttle and took off for home.

Darkness was closing in, and it had begun snowing heavily by the time Ezra reached MacDowell Lake. He decided to play it safe and spend the night there with Christian friends. Before landing, he announced his change of plans on the radio frequency used

^ Ezra stayed at his friend Johnny Kenequanash's house at MacDowell Lake on a number of occasions.

by mission stations. "Victor Tango Uniform[3] is landing because of heavy snow."

The next day was Sunday, and Ezra stayed for a church service with the small group of believers at MacDowell Lake. After the service and a meal, he was finally in the air. But by that time the weather was already deteriorating. Before long he was flying in light snow. As the minutes continued to tick by, the snowfall grew heavier. It was not long before Ezra knew it was unsafe to keep flying. He found a lake, circled around, and landed near the shore. A few minutes later visibility was reduced to practically zero, and

---

[3] VTU were the letters identifying Ezra's airplane registration. When pilots communicate by radio, they use words (one corresponding to each letter in the alphabet) to identify themselves, in an effort to be clearly understood.

Ezra was especially grateful to be safely on the lake.

Ezra remembered his unexpected camping trip with Elijah Stoney years earlier. Now Ezra was by himself. He remembered some of the things he had learned from the former experience and set about preparing for a night in the bush. First he took an axe and cut pine branches to fashion into a crude lean-to. He placed pine boughs on top of the snow in the shelter and then rolled out the warm sleeping bag that was kept in the airplane for emergencies just like this. Then he built a cheery fire and gathered an adequate supply of firewood for the night.

Now, what shall I eat? Ezra thought. He extracted a few items from the emergency supplies carried in the rear of the plane. *That's right*, he remembered. *I have that box of moose meat that was sent along for David Kakegamic.* Ezra knew David well and was certain he would be glad if Ezra would eat some of the meat.

Ezra took the axe and chopped off pieces of meat from the frozen package. He melted snow in a kettle and added the moose meat and some emergency food. He made a big bowlful of food, knowing he needed lots of calories to stay warm overnight. While he would have preferred being home with Nannie, Ezra was grateful for a full stomach, a warm fire, and adequate shelter.

The next morning it was still snowing enough that Ezra decided to stay where he was. At one point in the day he saw a plane in the distance and tried to call on the radio. Glen Roth was flying that plane, but he didn't hear Ezra because of a faulty radio. Ezra spent the second night in the bush.

By Tuesday morning several planes were looking for Ezra, in

^ Ezra and MIC's Cessna 180 on Howey Bay near Whitey Hostetler's hangar.

spite of poor flying conditions. The weather at Ezra's location seemed to be improving a bit, so he took off for home. A few minutes later he flew into heavier snowfall and was forced to land. Ezra called on the radio but no one heard him.

Ezra calculated that he still had enough gas for takeoff and the flight home, but if he had to land again before home, he would not have enough fuel for another takeoff. When visibility improved a short time later, he warmed the Cessna in preparation for departure. He radioed his location and intention of making one more attempt to get closer to Red Lake. Jim Yutzy, one of Northern Light Gospel Mission's pilots who was out looking for Ezra, had also been forced down by bad weather and was nearby, at Stormer Lake. He heard Ezra's radio transmission and radioed back, "Stay where you are. I will bring you some gas from Stormer Lake."

Jim soon arrived and helped Ezra refuel his plane. Both pilots took off for Red Lake and radioed their progress to the NLGM office. The office soon radioed back that the visibility there was zero-zero. The pilots diverted to Stormer Lake, where they made lunch and waited for better conditions. Finally, later in the afternoon, the weather had improved sufficiently for Ezra to make it home.

A young man was helping Ezra prepare to haul a load of gasoline into Bearskin Lake. Ezra told the young man not to fill the ten-gallon drums completely, but to leave space for the fuel to expand. By the time Ezra had the plane ready for departure, his

^ Ezra prepares to fly fuel to Bearskin Lake.

friend had the drums filled and the bungs[4] tightened. Together they secured the drums in the Cessna.

It was a beautiful summer day, and Ezra was enjoying the flight to Bearskin Lake. He decided to climb higher in the sky for an even broader view of the bush country over which he was flying.

As Ezra was nearing Muskrat Dam, he could smell gas. *Why am I smelling gas in the cabin?* he wondered.

He turned his head to survey the gasoline drums behind him and was alarmed to see gas floating around inside the rim of one drum. Apparently the drum had been filled too full, and the difference in the air pressure high above the ground had forced gas out of the barrel. The smell of gasoline was strong in the airplane. Ezra ventilated the cabin as quickly as he could and turned off any electronics that could cause a spark. He descended slowly into Bearskin Lake and landed safely. One spark in the cabin could have blown up the airplane. God was gracious!

---

[4] Screw-in closures used to seal a barrel.

22
EXPANDING THE WORK

In the 1960s, Mission Interests Committee sought to broaden its Gospel outreach in the North.

In 1963, William and Lucy Yoder moved to Ignace, Ontario, to take up an outreach begun earlier by Moses and Sadie Mast. The Yoders held both Sunday school and church services there. They also began Sunday schools in the nearby towns of Dyment, Valora, and Umfreville.

In April 1964, David and Esther Herschberger arrived in Red Lake. MIC was looking for a new place to proclaim the Gospel, and David and Esther had a burden to help. One of the first things David and Esther did was to enroll in a language course. Throughout the following summer, Ezra and David made several trips in hopes of finding a suitable location for the Herschberger family to start an outreach.

Mine Centre was one of their destinations. Mine Centre was a native settlement located between Atikokan and Fort Francis. In 1964 there was no road connecting Mine Centre to the rest of the world. Travel was best done by water.

In those days Christian workers known as Shantymen were busy throughout the northland doing itinerant evangelistic work. They would travel to isolated communities and logging camps to share the Gospel message and distribute Bibles and Christian literature. The lumberjacks who lived in the logging camps often lived in small, rustic shanties, many of which were quite crude. The itinerant Christian workers shared the rough living standards of the lumberjacks. So when the loggers saw the traveling preachers coming to stay with them for a while, they would call to each other, "Here come the Shantymen!" The name stuck.

Ezra and David made contact with some Shantymen to inquire about the advisability of opening a regular Christian witness in Mine Centre. The Shantymen made inquiries in that village and reported a favorable response back to the MIC men. They even offered to accompany the mission men on their initial visit and make the necessary introductions to the village leaders.

"It looks like we are going to have quite a trip," observed David as he and Ezra finished packing food and other supplies into the station wagon.

"We need to be prepared to be gone about three days," Ezra answered. "Not knowing where we will be each night, I thought it best to take our sleeping bags. We'll likely be roughing it at times." He paused. "I think we're ready for the canoe now. You grab the front, and I'll get the back. We'll flip it over and tie it down on top of the car. Ready?"

The men finished their task and double-checked all the ropes holding the canoe. They joined their wives for a farewell prayer, and then it was time to go.

Ezra and David left Red Lake and traveled south to the Trans-Canada Highway at Vermillion Bay. There they turned east. By nightfall they had made it as far as Ignace. William and Lucy were happy to see the men and provide overnight lodging for them.

Two Shantymen joined Ezra and David in the morning and together they headed for Atikokan, the last settlement on the road in the direction of Mine Centre. The older of the two Shantymen had plenty of interesting experiences and stories to relate from his years of itinerant preaching. Time passed quickly, and soon they could see the dam on the outskirts of Atikokan.

"I think we should take our lunch break now," Ezra announced. "It will be easier now than later when we are on the water. What do you think?"

"That sounds good to me," David agreed.

After lunch, they drove to the dam that would mark the end of their travel by car. The four men got out of the station wagon and took a look. The embankment from the road down to the water was very steep. "We need to carry the canoe down that bank and then load our belongings into it," Ezra announced.

It can't be done, David thought in dismay as he pondered the scene before him. But after multiple trips up and down that slope, the motor, gasoline, food, water, sleeping bags, and paddles were all safely stowed in the canoe. After four grown men got in, the canoe was loaded to the hilt. Heading downriver, they sometimes encountered rushing water, but since they were following the current, they had no problems.

Ezra was in the back of the canoe running the three-horsepower motor. The two Shantymen sat in the middle, and David occupied the front seat. The ride was smooth and relaxing. David was thoroughly enthralled as he drank in the ever-changing view from the prow.

A pair of mallards rose sharply on flapping wings from the water as the approaching canoe startled them. Their quacks were audible above the noise of the motor. Farther on, they passed a beaver's house, a large mound made of sticks and mud.

After some time they spotted the village on the north shore of the river. Some boats were tied by the dock. Ezra steered the canoe along one side of the dock and eased it onto the shore. No one was around. The men climbed out and stretched their cramped muscles. They walked up the grass-lined pathway. The trail, obviously a well-used path, led them to the top of a rise where the village school stood. The elder Shantyman had been to this village before, and he led the way into the school.

They soon discovered they were not the only visitors in Mine Centre. A Roman Catholic priest was also there.

"Does this mean our trip is in vain?" David quietly asked Ezra when they were alone for a few minutes. "Are we defeated before we have even begun?"

"Oh, I don't know about that," Ezra replied. "The Shantyman doesn't seem too disturbed by the priest's presence. He simply told the priest that we were visiting isolated communities and are prepared to have a short Christian program this evening. If I heard correctly, the priest and the school teacher agreed that would be a good idea. The teacher voiced his opinion that the community people would enjoy that."

Many community people did come out for the service. David noticed that the people seemed shy and reserved. Both the older Shantyman and Ezra had opportunity to speak with the people. David was content to stay in the background and pray about the contacts that were being made.

With the priest present, Ezra realized that it was unwise to speak of stationing a mission couple there. In the end, though, both David and Ezra agreed it had been a good contact and a worthwhile visit. After the community people had gone home, the men spread out their sleeping bags in the school building and slept there for the night.

In the morning, the men ate their breakfast and were ready to leave by the time the teacher and students arrived. As they loaded the canoe for their return trip, Ezra had some advice. "On the way back to the car, we're going upstream. We'll likely have to paddle sometimes because the outboard motor isn't strong enough to propel us through swift water. It's important to have the canoe balanced so that it doesn't tip over. Let's load the canoe with the heavy items low and evenly distributed."

When all their gear was satisfactorily stowed and the canoe was ready to leave the shore, Ezra took his place in the back end and the two Shantymen got in the middle. It was David's job to launch their craft from shore. He grabbed the canoe with both hands and gave a smooth, forceful push out into the river. At just the right moment, he jumped and landed with his knees on the prow. Landing too early would have grounded the front of the canoe in the shallow water. Jumping too late, he would have gotten wet. On this occasion, David timed his movements perfectly. All that remained was to go from his perch on top of the canoe to a seated position facing the front, which also required keeping his center of gravity low and evenly balanced.

"Well done," Ezra said as David took his seat. With that, Ezra started the motor and headed upstream for Atikokan.

The first stretch was no problem. When they came to a narrows with swifter current, though, the limitations of their small motor became starkly evident. The motor was running wide open, but its force was matched by the opposing force of the oncoming current. They came to a halt. David and the Shantymen grabbed paddles and tried to keep the boat from turning broadside in the rushing current.

"Paddle forward, all three of you," Ezra called urgently from the back. Backs and shoulders bent to the task as the men paddled with all their strength. Slowly the canoe began inching forward against the rushing water. From his perch in the back with his hand on the tiller, Ezra could see the men pulling. The situation was tense, and the paddler's arms ached as they slowly made progress through the swift water. Several minutes later the men were happy to lay their paddles aside as the motor was again able to propel them upstream.

They arrived back at the dam with little more difficulty. Then everything had to be carried up the steep bank. Here they parted ways. While Ezra and David would be driving back to Red Lake, the Shantymen would be heading for the next town on their route to share the Gospel. Ezra thanked the men for accompanying them on the trip and introducing them to the people of Mine Centre.

Ezra and David had many things to discuss as they travelled back to Red Lake. Later, as they reflected on what they had learned, they concluded that God was not leading them to Mine Centre at that time. To station a family there would require communication equipment the mission did not possess. Transportation to and from Mine Centre would be difficult, although it could be done. In the end, Ezra and David believed God was directing them to consider other options.

Not long after that trip, Ezra received a message from Morris Thomas, a man from the Lac Seul reserve, southeast of Red Lake. The gist of the message was this: "Please come to Lac Seul and help us start a church like you have at Red Lake."

Ezra and David again prepared for a trip. Instead of a canoe, they would be using Ezra's boat. A local man agreed to go along as a guide since he was knowledgeable about the lakes they would be passing through.

The morning of the trip, David arrived at Ezra's house before daylight. They had to leave early to reach Lac Seul by noon. The shining stars and light winds promised a good start to their trip.

"Good morning, Ezra!"

"Good morning to you, David," Ezra replied. "It's a good morning, but I have disappointing news."

"What is that?" David sounded worried.

"Our guide has changed his mind about going along," Ezra explained.

"Oh, no!" David's disappointment was keen. "Does this mean that we aren't going?"

"Not at all," Ezra answered. "We will go anyway. I have a map, and I believe we can find our way."

Together the men went over a checklist of items necessary for their trip. One important item was a compass to assist them in traveling through unfamiliar water. Ezra's boat and trailer were already hitched behind the station wagon. Before long they were headed down Route 605 to Ear Falls, seventy-two kilometers away. They crossed the dam at Ear Falls and launched their boat into the light, choppy waters of the sprawling Lac Seul Lake.

Navigation was a major issue when traversing such a lake. Their destination was over forty miles away, across a large body of water sprinkled with many dozens of islands, large and small. It was no small task keeping track of the changing land masses. Ezra steered the boat while David spread out the map on the boat seat. Together they held a running dialogue.

"Which side of that island do I go around?" Ezra asked.

"The left side looks the most direct," David said. "Then when we get through the narrows, we will need to bear to the right."

"Keep an eye out for rocks," Ezra cautioned. "The ones sticking above the water are obvious. The rocks just below the surface are the ones that can mess up our trip in a hurry."

"How do I keep an eye out for them?" David wanted to know.

"One way is to closely observe the surface of the water ahead," Ezra explained. "Watch for subtle changes in the appearance of the waves. That often gives a clue that something is just below the surface."

"Ok, I'll try that," said David. "By the way, do you see that point up ahead on the right? I think it is here," he said, indicating the spot on the map. "If this is correct, around that point will be a bay with a sharp corner in it."

"You are doing a good job keeping track," Ezra acknowledged. "Looks like a stretch of open water ahead. Let's see, which opening should I head for?"

For two and a half hours they navigated by map and compass until they came into the vicinity of Kejick Bay Island, where the main Lac Seul settlement was located.

How do we find the people we need to speak to? was the question that lay heavily on both their minds. They saw the store and a few houses and decided to ask for directions.

"Boozhoo," they greeted a man near the shore. "Can you tell us where we can find Morris Thomas?"

The man nodded and indicated that Morris lived about two miles farther. "But," he added, "David Angecaneb lives in this bay, just a few houses away. He is one of our village council members. You might want to visit him."

Ezra and David took the opportunity to meet David Angecaneb and explained their desire to share the Gospel in the Lac Seul area. David was very glad to see them and hear the purpose of their visit. He welcomed them to come as soon as possible and also gave them the name of another council member, James, who lived across the bay. That visit proved less satisfactory. James was not as welcoming and expressed his opinion that they had all the spiritual help they needed for now.

"That gives me a letdown feeling," David said as they stopped to eat their lunch a bit farther down the shore. "It seemed earlier that the doors here were wide open. Now I'm not so sure."

After lunch they motored across the bay, hoping to meet Morris Thomas. A group of people gathered to see who they were. Morris was among them. Ezra and David were delighted to finally meet him. Morris welcomed them to come to his house to visit.

It was a warm summer day, so chairs and benches were carried outside where it was cooler. They visited for a while. Soon John Bull, the chief, came walking down the hill. He had a big smile on his face and welcomed the men to Lac Seul.

"We really need your help," John explained. "The minister who was here is gone. How soon can you come and help us with Sunday services?"

A long discussion followed as to how the mission might be able to handle their request.

"What housing is available here?" Ezra and David wanted to know.

The village leaders considered that question and talked among themselves for several minutes before answering. "We are not sure what would be available at this time."

"Would the people here be able to assist us in any way?" David asked.

"Oh, yes," the answer came quickly. "Most of us fish and hunt, and it is our custom to share what we get. We would be happy to give you fish and moose meat."

It seemed to Ezra and David that everyone at the meeting welcomed the possibility of David's family moving there. They were willing to help in any way they could. Quite a crowd had gathered to listen and add comments from time to time.

After several hours of discussion, Ezra turned to his fellow worker. "David, I think we should soon be heading home."

"I agree," David said. "We certainly don't want to navigate Lac Seul in the dark."

There were handshakes and goodbyes all around. Ezra and David sensed a genuine welcome and openness for direct spiritual work among the people. It seemed that God was opening a door to witness there. As they started on their return trip, both men expressed their gratefulness to God for His guidance and direction that day.

When they arrived back at Ear Falls, David and Ezra loaded the boat onto the trailer and headed up the road to Red Lake. They were glad to be home after a long day on the lake.

A full report of the trip to Lac Seul was given to their families and to the MIC board. After receiving their counsel and through a lot of consideration and prayer, it was decided that the Herschbergers should locate close enough to Lac Seul to be able to regularly minister there.

David and Ezra made several other trips to Lac Seul with Nannie and Esther accompanying them. Through these trips, they decided that David's family would settle in the neighboring town of Hudson. Living in Hudson would provide a lot of contact with Lac Seul people who came there to shop and do business. It was close enough to Lac Seul that David and Esther could minister in the Lac Seul settlement as well. God's leading had been evident, and it was with grateful hearts that David and Esther and their family began their many years of service in that part of God's vineyard.

23
LEARNING PROPER RESERVE

The early pioneers of mission work in Red Lake did not have the benefit of staff orientations that became commonplace later. They grew up in an era when many people were reluctant to speak publicly and instruct those of the opposite gender in matters of personal decorum. Following are accounts of three vulnerable missionaries in the North who learned these lessons in uncomfortable ways. They have humbly shared these timeless and universal lessons for the reader's instruction and benefit. It is precious to observe how God preserved the honor of His holy name and work in spite of the naiveté of His servants.

Paul Miller Remembers
Martha and I had been living at Round Lake two years, and I was teaching in a provincial school. God had already blessed our home with Hilda, Eldo, and Margaret. We were expecting our fourth child.

Martha and I have an Rh factor incompatibility in our blood.

This has the potential to cause serious problems for our newborn babies. The doctors had warned us that we have a 10 percent chance of a baby with a life-threatening disease in its blood because of this Rh factor incompatibility. They were adamant that Martha not give birth in the bush, far away from medical care. Because of this, we planned for her to fly out to Red Lake a month before she was due.

Martha and I discussed how I could fulfill my teaching responsibility and still care for our young children at home. We decided to hire a Christian lady to help us. She would do the laundry, cook, and care for our children while Martha was gone. Leona Beachy was a godly young lady from Ohio who consented to come help our family.

Prior to Leona's arrival, I was sharing our supposedly well-thought-out plans with the local Baptist missionary at Round Lake. He was more perceptive than I was about how such a situation would be viewed and shared a warning with me. "If your wife goes to Red Lake and your hired girl sleeps in your house at night, some in the village will conclude that you two sleep together."

That was a great shock to me, and I was deeply troubled that our Christian witness for the Lord could be compromised. We needed Leona's help, but certainly something in our plans needed to change. As the pastor and I discussed my predicament, we came up with the idea to ask Jenny Kakegamic, a girl from the community, to come to our house at night to be with Leona. Jenny was willing to come, and through her the Lord provided a way that we did not bring reproach upon the name of Christ.

Ezra Peachey Remembers

I was visiting one day, and I stopped at David and Greta Mosquito's house. Greta was there with some of her children. David was not yet home from work. I began discussing the Christian woman's veiling with Greta. She had some thoughts and questions, and I was doing my best to answer them. About that time, her husband arrived home from work and stepped through the doorway.

I immediately saw that David was very upset. I did not understand why. In the awkwardness of those moments it seemed best to leave, so I did. Nannie and I talked it over, and we concluded that it was inappropriate for me, being alone, to visit with a woman who was not my wife, even with her children present. We had been aware of immorality going on in some homes. Things like wife-swapping were taking place. A Christian had even asked me one time whether Christians should take part in wife-swapping. Some of our staff told of visiting a woman in her home one evening. Her husband was gone, and another man was in the house. From every indication, he was there for the night.

David never did say anything to me about what had happened. God taught me to be very discreet and not allow myself to get into that kind of situation again.

Wayne Schrock Remembers

My wife, Edna, and I were scheduled to leave one afternoon for a mission meeting with the Peacheys and Herschbergers in Red Lake. That morning I had an intuitive impression that I should visit Andy and Nancy Fobester. They lived in a little house about twelve miles out of Sioux Lookout. As the day wore on, I felt a stronger and stronger sense that I should visit them. Finally I told Edna that I had to go. I hoped to be back in time to make it to the mission meeting.

This was in the dead of winter. Three- to four-foot snow banks lined the roads. I had covered about half the distance to their house when it happened. As I came around a corner to the right, I slowly but surely got pulled into the snow bank. I was stuck—very stuck. The more I tried to get out, the deeper my vehicle sank into the ditch. Eventually I realized I would not get out without help. I resigned myself to waiting, reading Scripture, and praying that God would send someone to pull me out.

There was little traffic on that road. One man who did see me, however, stopped, saw how securely I was "in" and remarked, "Oh, I wish I had something to pull you out, but I don't." The man left and didn't return.

I was sitting there for a couple of hours when the thought suddenly struck me that maybe I wasn't supposed to be visiting the Fobesters until Andy got home from work. Yes, Nancy would probably be at home alone, and it would be inappropriate for me to drop in and visit with her at home alone.

And then I started laughing and laughing. I was laughing to the Lord for how He had put the brakes on my travels. The Lord impressed me with this thought: *I know how this is going to work out. At about 4:30 this afternoon someone is going to come along. They will have a chain, and they will be able to pull me out.*

That is exactly what happened. I was not surprised when a Good Samaritan showed up about half past four and pulled me out of the snow bank. I steered my vehicle more carefully, and when I drove into sight of the Fobesters' place, Andy was just walking up to his house, having arrived home from work.

We had a short visit, because it was getting late and I knew Edna would be wondering where I was. I did get home safely that evening, but it was too late to travel to Red Lake for the meeting. I thanked God for the powerful lesson He taught me that day. Experiencing the Lord's leading and protection meant a great deal to me. It affirmed that God's hand was present in that day's circumstances. Such experiences are priceless!

24
STUCK IN THE SLUSH

Slush on lakes was often a problem in the Canadian North. Slush formed when the weight of snow on a lake pushed the ice down enough so that the water beneath could flow through cracks in the ice. That water mixed with the snow on top of the ice, forming slush. Sometimes the layer of slush would be only several inches deep and the top would freeze into a crust. Other times the layer of slush would be thicker and the snow covering the slush remained soft and fluffy, insulating the slush below and keeping it from freezing.

Sometimes an alert snowmobile operator or airplane pilot would spot a shade of darkening in the snow ahead and avoid what was almost certainly slush. At other times, though, there was no indication of slush until a "dropping through" sensation was felt. When that happened, forward motion was suddenly slowed.

A wise driver who found himself in slush responded instantly with full power and an attempt to get away. Too often, it seemed, the snowmobile became so bogged down in the slushy mix that it would stop. While the ice beneath the slush was generally thick enough to bear the weight of the snowmobile and nothing would disappear into the lake, there was nothing safe about getting one's feet wet in slush when the temperature was twenty or thirty degrees below zero (Fahrenheit).

Ezra and his sons enjoyed trapping. One day he was out on the snowmobile checking the traps. Twice he got stuck in slush but was able to get out. Ezra rode on to Sadler Bay to check a couple of traps. As he turned to leave the bay, he felt the unmistakable signs of getting bogged down in slush again. He immediately applied full throttle, but the slush was too deep. In short order, he and the sled he was pulling were stuck.

Ezra first unhooked the sled and tried to drive the snowmobile out of the wet slop. No success. Ezra tried lifting the snowmobile out of the slush onto firmer snow, but he wasn't strong enough to do so. So, Ezra tried something else. He went ahead of the machine and began tramping the snow down into the slush. In those bitterly cold temperatures, the slush would firm up and freeze quickly, thus making a path for his snowmobile to get out of the slush.

Ezra had not been working long at this, however, when he realized he should stop. He knew his heart was weak, and it would not be wise to subject it to an extended time of tramping snow into the slush in this cold weather.

Ezra decided to wait for help. He had a brand new axe with him, though, and while he was waiting, he decided to make a fire to keep himself warm. He slowly plowed a path through the snow over to the edge of the lake where the top of a tall pine had snapped off and was lying in the snow. The tree top was good, dry wood; Ezra was looking forward to a nice fire. He decided to chop some knots out of the wood, because the knots contained more resin and would make a hotter fire than just the pine wood. When the axe hit the first knot, however, it made a funny sound. Ezra swung the second time, and it became clear that the axe was not biting into the wood.

Ezra lifted the axe to take a close look at the blade. It was, after all, a new axe, and Ezra was puzzled. He ran his hand over the blade and discovered something he had never seen before. The center of the blade was bent sideways. Apparently the metal was of an inferior quality or had not been hardened properly. When Ezra had purchased the axe, he had checked it out carefully. The axe had seemed like a good one in the store. Ezra recalled his deliberations at the time; he had decided against buying a good quality, German-forged axe for fifty dollars in favor of this cheaper one for fifteen dollars. Ezra had obviously made the wrong decision, and now the axe he was holding was practically worthless.

Ezra was finally able to get a fire going using smaller twigs instead of pine knots. Although the axe would not cut, it still could knock off medium-sized branches. Ezra kept busy tending his fire as the sun slipped below the horizon, and darkness took over.

By that time, Nannie knew Ezra should have returned. She called their son, Nathaniel, who came to get the other snowmobile. He filled it up with gas and headed out to the trapline. He followed Ezra's snowmobile tracks until they turned into a bay. Then he cut directly across the mouth of the bay until he intercepted Ezra's tracks coming out. That way Nathaniel could quickly conclude that his father was not somewhere back in that bay. Nathaniel also found the places where Ezra had gotten stuck in the slush.

When Nathaniel entered Sadler Bay, he noted his father's fire and was soon beside Ezra. They went over to Ezra's snowmobile and were pleased to discover it had not yet completely frozen in. Before long, they had the machine out of the slush, the sled hooked on, and they were headed for home.

That incident taught Ezra another lesson. A dependable, sharp axe is very valuable when a person is stranded in the bush. Relying on an inferior quality axe was inconvenient at best and dangerous at worst. The quality of an axe is not so accurately perceived by its attractiveness on the store rack as in the axe's ability to perform the duty for which it is made. Ezra discovered the hard way that the bargain axe was no bargain at all. These kinds of personal experiences provided illustrations for teaching deep truths from the Bible.

25
FINANCES

During his tenure in the North, Ezra often found himself assisting in the financial matters of various people. Sometimes people would come to him, requesting help to make their income last until the next check. At other times, family, social workers, and even the government would ask Ezra to assist those who were not able to control their spending. Helping people in the role of a financial trustee involved careful record keeping. It also provided frequent interactions with neighbors as the regular disbursements were made.

A man named Tommy[1] approached Ezra one day. "I would like you to help me," he began.

"How can I help you?" Ezra questioned.

"It is too easy to spend my paycheck on booze," Tommy replied. "I am hoping you will keep my earnings for me, and I will have to come and ask for my money when I have a genuine need for

---

[1] Pseudonym used.

it. Doing that might make it easier for me not to yield in a weak moment and spend everything I have, only to regret it later."

"I will do that for you, Tommy," Ezra answered. "I hope doing this will be a blessing to you."

That continued successfully for some time, so Tommy wanted to return to keeping his own money. That proved to be too great a temptation, and Tommy soon was spending most of his income on liquor again.

Several widows gave their pension funds to Ezra for safekeeping from the demands of relatives. These women were grateful for a trustworthy person who would stand between them and family members who would try to put them on a guilt trip for not handing over any available money. Ezra took great care to ensure that all funds were accurately accounted for and disbursed properly.

Ezra was aware of several incidents where native people were awarded various financial settlements, but the payment was never received. At some personal risk, Ezra made the necessary inquiries and discovered that certain dishonest men were pocketing what was meant for their clients. When a dear Christian native lady, a friend of the Peacheys, was involved in an automobile accident, Ezra had a discussion with the lawyer in charge of the case. Ezra remembered those previous occasions of fraud, and he wanted to make sure nobody took advantage of the lady. In the end, the lawyer sent the settlement check to Ezra, in Ezra's name, and Ezra was required to have someone witness him signing the check to transfer the money to the lady.

When Ezra and Nannie went to visit their friend at the hospital in Winnipeg, Ezra took the check along. At the hospital, he requested that someone in authority witness the signing procedure. The hospital administration explained that they weren't involved in those types of dealings, but they called in a social worker. The social worker was also keenly aware of unscrupulous people who tried to take advantage of native clients.

"Why are you handling this lady's money?" she demanded of Ezra.

"Ask her," Ezra replied.

"Why is this man taking care of your money?" the social worker then asked the lady.

"If this money is sent to my husband, it will be gone before I get home," she replied. "I know this man. He is my pastor. He will use the funds as they are supposed to be used. I trust him."

That was sufficient confirmation for the social worker to witness the signing of the check. Ezra then kept the lady's money for her and carefully recorded all disbursements to the lady over the next five or six years. Eventually the lady chose to handle the rest of her funds, and Ezra relieved himself of that particular responsibility.

These kinds of trustworthy services to the native people endeared the Peacheys to many.

26
RECOLLECTIONS OF SERVICE

Wayne Schrock first came to Red Lake in 1961 as a single man to do carpentry work for Northern Light Gospel Mission. He recalls: "I was downstairs with Irwin and Susan Schantz when Ezra came in. He wanted to talk with Irwin about something he had just observed about the native people. Ezra was enthusiastic and had a drive to understand the culture of the people to whom he was called to minister. I decided to attend the Wednesday evening Bible study held at Red Lake Indian School."

Knowing mere smatterings of the birth pains of MIC's work at Red Lake, Wayne was impressed by the number of native people who came to receive Bible teaching that night. What had begun as an institution to provide schooling for underprivileged children had somewhat inadvertently developed into a local church, composed primarily of native people.

As Wayne considered what he observed, he marked the enthusiasm of those early workers to preach and teach about the fire that was burning in their own hearts. The sacred flame that sparked a revival in American Amish circles during preceding years was now kindling a fire in Red Lake. Wayne remembers the thoughts impressed upon his mind that evening. *These people are on fire for the Lord, and through their enthusiastic, grateful service toward their Master, souls are being saved and discipled in the ways of the kingdom of God.*

Ten years later, Wayne returned to the North as a married man. This time he worked under MIC. Following are some of his recollections about his time in the North:

> When Edna and I moved to Sioux Lookout in 1971, there was a well-established church group at Red Lake. Ezra had mentored several men as pastors: John Mamakeesic, David Mosquito, Elijah Beardy, and later Jimmy Meekis. They had a good thing going there.
>
> David and Elijah and their families eventually moved back to Bearskin to spread the Gospel among the people of their home reserve. Later, John returned home to Sandy Lake and faithfully ministered the Gospel there for the rest of his life. About the same time, the Pentecostal movement swept through much of the North and the leaders of the movement drew many into their fold, including a number from the church at the Red Lake Indian School. From then on, building a local native church at Red Lake was always a struggle. While they continued to have services at Red Lake, the group did not develop into an established church with committed membership.

After the school had closed and some of the key men had returned to their far-flung northern reserves, Ezra began to focus on periodically holding Bible schools at the school building and, more important, on visiting the native leaders in their home settings.

Once, Ezra invited me along on a trip to Bearskin, and I considered that a privilege. While my work at the time was in Sioux Lookout, that Bearskin trip gave me a glimpse into life in those isolated villages. It also opened a window into how Ezra conducted his work.

I drove to Red Lake and flew with Ezra from there in MIC's Cessna 180. I observed that Ezra was a cautious pilot. He was very calculated and didn't take chances.

The weather was good for flying a floatplane that day. When we landed at Bearskin, I was impressed as the men came down to meet us at the dock. I could tell they appreciated Ezra, even those who were not Christians. They all crowded around him. We ended up at David Mosquito's house and enjoyed their hospitality. Greta didn't try to cater to us and make white man's food. Rather, she served us what they had to eat. Our meal was largely moose meat and bannock.

I noted with interest that Ezra was not pushy about having a service. He left it up to David to decide whether we would have one. David finally decided to have a meeting and invited people to the house. About fifteen people came, and we sat around in the Mosquitos' living room. David asked Ezra to speak and asked me for a word of testimony, both spoken through an interpreter.

I still remember that Ezra spoke about dreams and visions. Native people put a lot of stock in those things. Ezra referred to the Old Testament and what the Bible says about those who have visions and dreams. "If what they say doesn't come to pass, you know their teachings are false." In a didactic and thorough manner, he went through the Scriptures, making practical applications.

We stayed in Bearskin overnight. The next morning we flew back to Red Lake.

One of the things I learned from Ezra was the importance of storytelling in preaching and teaching. If you want to communicate to indigenous peoples, you have to tell stories. I have frequently heard native pastors preach a one-point sermon. Those native pastors go all around that one point with stories, illustrations, and Bible verses. Ezra was known for teaching in the same manner.

I recall how various mission and native church leaders met in the late '80s and early '90s to discuss how missions might best help the native leaders in their spiritual labors. We explored ways by which the outreaches started by missionaries might be turned over to the native leaders. One thing in particular stood out to me during those several days together. We had asked the native brethren how we could help them. They answered by asking us to come around to the outreaches to teach and preach for them. When we asked them whom we should send, they answered by pointing their lips at Ezra and saying, "Send Ezra."

I believe they responded that way because Ezra was effective in communicating on their level. He couldn't speak the language like some other workers could, but he had the ability to speak in a way that they could understand. Ezra was not a flashy or charismatic speaker. He was more thoughtful and stoic in his manner of delivery. But what he said was well thought through and intellectually sound. Those things made the people comfortable.

It is interesting to me to note Ezra's life-changing experience in Central America, where a burden for the souls of lost men came profoundly upon him. That is where the same burden was pressed deeply into my own heart.

I was working in El Savador at the time under Amish-Mennonite Aid, and a missionary friend and I were driving back to Sitio Del Niño, a town near the national capital. We drove through a Catholic village on Good Friday, and the townspeople were reenacting the burial of Christ. The main road through the village was full of people in a procession. We were forced off the road and had to park. Hundreds of people, all dressed in black, were carrying candles and chanting mournfully as they followed a statue of the dead Christ being carried ahead of them. Observing this multitude of people and hearing the march of their feet was an arresting moment for me. I saw and understood that these people, these religious people, were lost. They were seeking for something to satisfy, a kind of religiosity. That was where I felt my first call to missions.

Later during my time in El Salvador, John Glick and I went to Guatemala for a week of vacation. We went to Chichicastenango, a beautiful city inhabited by many Quiche Indians. The Catholic Church had tried to proselytize these people, and the resulting religion was a mixture of Catholicism and the indigenous religion. We were touched to see these people coming to the altar in the front of the church. There they would perform their rituals.

The thing that impressed me most, though, happened on a high hill outside the city. I had left our cheap hotel room very early one morning and hiked to a shrine on top of this nearby hill. There I observed two Quiche people in front of that shrine. They were performing rituals and sacrifices, chanting as they tried to get in touch with God. I stood somewhat hidden behind a tree, as I didn't want to intrude, but I watched what was going on. It was probably the most defining moment in my life. I felt God's call in a more definite way to share the Gospel.

It is interesting that for both Ezra and me, our sense of call began in the South and led us to the North. May the name of the Lord Jesus Christ be praised!

27
GOD PROVIDES

Late September breezes rippled the clear, deep waters of Red Lake. A brilliant sun slowly traced its lowering arc across the afternoon sky. Birch and poplar trees were topped with variegated crowns of green and gold, their drying leaves rustling soothingly. Occasionally a stronger gust of wind would unburden the limbs, sending a shower of leaves fluttering softly to the carpeted ground below. A towering white pine, resplendent in five-needle clusters, stood silently, like a sentry on the rocky ridge, surveying the tamarack trading its summer green coat for autumn needles of burnished gold. Between water and trees, ancient granite outcroppings rose like a barrier, as if protecting the one from the other.

Near the shore in one of Red Lake's bays, Ezra sat quietly in his cedar strip canoe, paddle resting lightly across his lap. It was hunting season, and he was hoping to shoot a moose to provide meat for the coming winter. Ezra had planned to hunt a different place today, but the wind would have pushed his scent into the area ahead of him. Instead, he had paddled stealthily into Muskrat

Bay, where he could be downwind of the place he wanted to watch. Years of practice enabled him to withdraw his paddle soundlessly, sweep it forward barely an inch above the surface, and reenter the water for the next stroke with scarcely a noise. As a hunter, he certainly did not want to announce his arrival. Although moose do not see well, they make up for that deficit with superb hearing and smelling.

Ezra had a lot of time to think as he waited and watched. The rhythmic lapping of water against the side of the canvas hull seemed to take him back, step by step, to the decision to come North. There certainly had been other options instead of coming to Red Lake. Back then, Nannie's father had offered them a farm in Pennsylvania for $35,000. Now, that very farm was worth three-quarters of a million dollars. God had called them to Red Lake, though, and they had come.

What did the coming years hold for Nannie and him? Their time in the North no longer stretched unendingly into the future. It seemed that God was leading them back to close relatives in Belleville, Pennsylvania. Just as the pronounced shades of gray had touched his hair, so the accumulation of birthdays had fingered the once-boundless strength of youth.

Ezra's thoughts turned to his dear wife, who was nine years his junior. *What will happen to her if I pass on before she does?* he wondered. *If death claims me first, how will she be provided for during the rest of her life?*

During their years in Red Lake, God had provided for them adequately and abundantly. Their focus had been on ministering to the souls of men and women rather than on laying up a nest egg for retirement. Ezra's thoughts turned in gratitude to God as he pondered God's faithfulness to them in the many situations they had encountered. *Yes, whenever we trusted God, we found Him to be completely trustworthy,* Ezra concluded. God would certainly be true to His promises wherever they lived. But right then, there was so much that was unknown!

As he waited for a moose, Ezra began talking to God, telling Him the thoughts and questions that weighed heavily on his mind. He spoke of how they had obeyed and trusted God all these years. He openly asked God the questions about provision for the future that he and Nannie had no way of answering. "Heavenly Father," he whispered, "Lord, would you give me a token of assurance that you will provide for us in the future?" Tears welled in his eyes as he continued, "As a token of your continued provision, would you send out a moose for us today?"

The thought came almost immediately to Ezra's mind, *Where should I go to be best prepared for the moose that is coming?* He decided to paddle to the middle of the small cove and wait there. Upwind, across one hundred fifty yards of open water, was a large area of tall grass where a moose might come to feed. A narrow strip of tag alders formed a dense barrier between the grass and the mature trees growing on higher ground, a few yards inland. It seemed this would be a good place to wait and watch.

A few minutes later Ezra's ears picked up the sound of chattering squirrels back in the bush. His heart quickened as he thought of the possibilities. First-hand experience had taught him that those little red squirrels often scold loudly when man or beast enters their territory. *Maybe a moose is causing them to chatter*, he reasoned hopefully. A few more minutes went by. Then Ezra heard the muffled crunch of twigs snapping under a heavy weight, and his heart beat even faster. The sounds were coming closer and getting louder. Next, he heard the unmistakable sound of shattering ice as something walked through iced-over water puddles. It just had to be a moose making those noises!

Ezra silently maneuvered the canoe to the best position for shooting. After quietly laying the paddle across the thwart, he picked up his rifle and waited expectantly. The noises were consistent and loud, and he hoped the moose would be a bull. His license didn't permit him to shoot a cow.

Ezra didn't have much longer to wait. The first thing he saw was a massive rack of antlers emerging from the tag alders and the grass. There it was, a huge bull moose, picking his way over the watery, grassy clumps. When it was in the clear, about one hundred fifty yards away from the canoe, the moose stood still, broadside to Ezra. He carefully aimed his 30-06 rifle and squeezed the trigger. The moose spun around one hundred eighty degrees and was again positioned broadside to the canoe by the time Ezra had bolted another round into the chamber. He shot at the moose the second time, and it turned back toward the tag alders. It walked about thirty feet and disappeared from view. "God answered my prayer, and I think I got that moose!" Ezra breathed in awe as he waited there a few minutes longer, listening.

Ezra heard the moose blow its nose a few times, but soon all was quiet. He traded gun for paddle and was soon paddling toward where he had last seen the moose. When Ezra entered a narrow, grass-free channel leading toward a beaver lodge he found his way blocked by a thick mat of poplar tree branches, a beaver's winter feed bed. Just beyond that obstacle, Ezra found the moose. Its front feet were up on a grass clump and the hind legs stuck in the lake bottom. The moose was dead.

As if on cue, Ezra heard the sound of an outboard motor coming into the bay. It was Kevin Miller, a fellow mission worker who had been hunting a short distance away. Kevin had heard the shots and came to investigate. When he saw Ezra waving his paddle, he came as close as he could and shut off the motor.

"Did you get your moose?" Kevin called out.

Ezra nodded his head in affirmation and yelled back, "Yes, I did. A big bull."

"Where is it?"

"Just beyond where I am," Ezra replied. "We won't be able to get the boat back in here. Let me come out in the canoe and get you."

In a few more minutes, both Ezra and Kevin were staring at the huge moose. They realized they could not possibly get him out of there in one piece. The antlers on top of the massive head and neck measured fifty-four inches across.

"Perhaps we will have to cut the head off if we hope to move this critter," Ezra suggested.

"You're probably right," agreed Kevin.

They slogged around the watery grass clumps, working hard to cut through the moose's huge muscles, and finally succeeded in severing the head from the body. Together, Ezra and Kevin carried the head to a grassy spot on the shore. Returning to the headless carcass, they pulled on the front legs until the hind legs were freed from the mucky bottom. The men then floated the carcass a short distance to the poplar branch feed bed and tried to pull it across.

"I don't think this is going to work," Kevin said.

"Let's pull it up against these branches," Ezra suggested. "Then we can try to roll him onto the feed bed by pulling on his legs."

"It's worth a try, Ezra," Kevin said, and they moved the moose onto the feed bed.

Still, they had to field dress the moose and get him over the feed bed to open water. Together they presented quite a picture. One elderly man without hip boots stood on the floating mass of poplar branches, trying to field dress a huge moose. A younger man stood in the canoe, trying to keep the moose from rolling back into the water. Of course, within a few minutes Ezra was soaked to the bone and his boots were full of water. Finally the moose's entrails were all removed.

"Now what?" Kevin asked.

"We have those long ropes in the boat," Ezra said. "If we tied one end to the moose and the other to the boat, do you think we could pull this carcass over the feed bed?"

The men attempted this several times, but the twenty-five horsepower motor of Kevin's boat simply churned the water and could not get the moose moving. Ezra and Kevin cut the moose in half crosswise and tried again. This time they were successful. As the first half of the moose slid into water on the bay side of the feed bed, Kevin opened the throttle on the outboard motor. Drawing near to a big flat rock out in the bay, Kevin idled the motor until the keel gently bumped the rock. Ezra climbed out and held the boat until Kevin could join him. Pulling together, they were able to drag the half moose up onto the rock. The men had to repeat this whole procedure for the other half of the moose. Then they cut the pieces into more manageable chunks. Finally, they returned to the kill site one last time to retrieve the head and antlers. Everything had to be taken to the rock for overnight storage.

"I'm ready to dry out and get some rest," Ezra declared as they pulled the boat up on shore in front of their trapping cabin a short while later. "I'm all tuckered out."

"You go right ahead and rest," Kevin volunteered. "I'll take care of putting our gear away, and then I'll make supper."

Later, two weary but grateful men ate their meal and retired for the night. The next morning they stowed their gear in the boat and motored over to the flat rock. They manhandled the pieces of moose into the boat. The head and antlers were placed on top. It was a heavily loaded boat that plowed toward home that morning.

Ezra and Kevin arrived home shortly before noon. Kevin's wife saw them approaching and came down to meet them at the dock. She offered to call Nannie, but Nannie didn't answer the phone. So Ezra started walking up the road toward home. As he neared their house, Nannie saw him.

"What are you doing, coming home so soon?" she wondered.

"Well, you come down to the dock and see what we have!" Ezra answered.

Although she normally was unflappable, Nannie became quite excited as they started toward the dock. When she saw the huge moose head on top of the pile of meat, she became really excited.

They took some pictures and then unloaded the meat. There

^ Kevin Miller and Ezra Peachy with the head of the big moose God sent in answer to Ezra's prayer.

was a tremendous amount of work ahead to prepare all that meat for storage.

"Thank you again, heavenly Father, for answered prayer," Ezra prayed that evening. "Thank you for sending the moose and helping me to get it. Thank you for giving Kevin and me the strength to bring it home. And thank you, too, for this token of your faithfulness."

◆ ◆

As Ezra and Nannie's move back to Belleville became imminent, MIC's field director, Darrell Nisly, was concerned about them. One day he talked with Ezra. "Ezra, when you move back to

Pennsylvania, do you have enough money to retire comfortably?"

Ezra thought for a bit. He had previously learned that their long service in Canada meant that very little income would be coming from American Social Security. He and Nannie would receive less than $150 per month. He answered Darrell, "Not unless we would continue to get an allowance from the mission."

Mission Interests Committee decided to put a notice in the February 2005 issue of the *Calvary Messenger*. A slightly edited version of the announcement appears here:

> To our brethren in the Lord,
>
> We extend greetings of peace and love in the wonderful name of the Lord Jesus, the one who is building His church. It is our privilege to be co-laborers with Him in the great task of bringing souls into His kingdom.
>
> The MIC board would like to inform you of a current need. We desire to provide satisfactory compensation for our long-term missionaries. Over the years, we have been giving a designated amount of what we call "retirement funds" to eligible workers. These funds are reserved for missionaries' retirement. However, we have not been able to accumulate enough funds to provide nearly the amount earned by today's average laborer.
>
> Ezra and Nannie Peachey, Red Lake, Ontario, have been serving with Believers' Fellowship[1] since 1959. They

---

[1] MIC church plants became officially identified as Believers' Fellowship in 1972.

have faithfully ministered to the indigenous people in Red Lake and in the hinterland beyond. For many years, Ezra served as administrator of Believers' Fellowship. He continues to provide valuable insight for fellow missionaries.

Ezra is now in his upper 70s with some health concerns, and the Peacheys feel led to move back to their home community of Belleville, Pennsylvania. This is not an easy decision for them. They have given most of their lives to serve the indigenous people in Ontario, and a part of their hearts will always remain in the North.

We would like to help them with their living expenses in retirement, so we are inviting you to share with them in a love offering for this purpose. They are planning to move back to Belleville in the spring of 2005, and we welcome your contributions at any time. Thank you and God bless you.

That notice resulted in a great outpouring of financial giving. Ezra and Nannie had the choice of receiving the total amount in one lump sum or in periodic disbursements. They chose the latter. Ezra and Nannie are very grateful to God and supporters of MIC for providing for them in this way.

The moose had been a token of God's continuing faithfulness for the coming years.

Ezra and Nannie moved home to Belleville, Pennsylvania, in 2005. Ezra's nephew fixed up his basement for them to live in. The local Valley View and Pleasant View Amish-Mennonite congregations expressed willingness to help Ezra and Nannie build a house. Other churches from as far away as Lancaster County, Pennsylvania, wanted to help too. Ezra had some money for a house, but not nearly enough for the whole project; they knew they would be relying on the Lord to finish the job.

The first big question was *where* to build. The Peacheys looked at various options and finally decided to buy a lot on Susan Drive. When the land was purchased, Ezra and Nannie walked around the whole parcel and dedicated it to the Lord.

"It is His," declared Ezra, "and we will build here as the Lord

^ Ezra and Nannie in 2013 on the Blue Ridge Mountains.

provides." Over the next months, the house took shape. Many, many people, both from the churches in the valley around Belleville and areas beyond, donated labor and materials. It was amazing to watch the house come together. It was truly a labor of love for the Lord and for the Peacheys.

Many times over the years, Ezra and Nannie had noticed the verses in Mark 10: 29–31. "And Jesus answered and said, Verily I say unto you, There is no man that hath left house, or brethren, or sisters, or father, or mother, or wife, or children, or lands, for my sake, and the gospel's, but he shall receive an hundredfold now in this time, houses, and brethren, and sisters, and mothers, and children, and lands, with persecutions; and in the world to come eternal life. But many that are first shall be last, and the last first."

Ezra and Nannie still reminisce about God's faithfulness to them through all their years in the North. They remember the food trucks that delivered gifts of love from friends and supporters. They remember prayers for wisdom and God's answers to their prayers. Countless times throughout those years, the Peacheys had been encouraged by a timely visit, an answer to prayer, or an unexpected gift.

Ezra shared with people in Belleville and in other local churches about the Peachey family's experiences in the North. Ezra was happy and grateful to relate how God had provided for them all those years. "We never suffered from unmet needs," he said.

At the time of the writing of this book, Ezra and Nannie have lived in Belleville for almost nine years. On a wall of their garage hang the massive moose antlers, a token of God's faithfulness in answer to Ezra's prayer. Month after month, the Peacheys are grateful all over again to God and His children who so generously provided funds on which they live.

"Many a time," Ezra testifies, "when we crest the knoll on Grandview Street and see our house ahead, we say, 'Isn't that a nice house the Lord gave us?'"

EPILOGUE

MIC's spiritual endeavors in the North have continued through the intervening years to the publishing of this book.

The outreach begun in Lac Seul and Hudson in 1964 with the David Herschberger family continues to the present. Frenchman's Head, Whitefish Bay, and Kejick Bay are three settlements in the greater Lac Seul Lake area where the Herschbergers and others have preached the Gospel, mentored Christians, and counseled many individuals and families. David and Esther also developed a Christian book and literature ministry that serves both the local communities and many of the northern reserves. Esther died suddenly in 1995 when a moose collided with the vehicle in which she and David were traveling. In 1997 David married Frieda Bontrager, who had served with the mission since 1974. She and David enjoyed sixteen years of marriage, serving the Lord together until David's passing late in 2013.

Wayne and Edna Schrock labored in Sioux Lookout for more than thirty years, teaching, doing church-planting work, and making disciples of new believers. Wayne also served as MIC's field director for twelve years. The Schrocks returned to Virginia in 2007.

The church plants started in Red Lake and Sioux Lookout continue to the present and are undergoing a transition away from MIC oversight. MIC continues its work in Sioux Narrows, with Darrell and Kathy Nisly leading in the work there. Darrell currently serves as MIC field director. Two families presently serve in Kenora. Their work includes evangelizing and holding Sunday school and church services.

Please pray for the MIC workers as they continue proclaiming the message of salvation to the lost in the North, especially ministering to the spiritual needs of the First Nations people.[1]

---

[1] "First Nations" is the current name by which the indigenous people of Canada prefer to be recognized.

ABOUT THE AUTHOR

Robert Stauffer (Bob) and his wife Doris reside in beautiful northern Minnesota on the shores of Popple Lake. They are grateful to God for the blessing of four children and fifteen grandchildren.

Bob grew up near Lancaster, Pennsylvania, on a small farm. He answered God's call to voluntary service in Ontario in 1970 and two years later married Doris. Together they spent ten more years serving in various roles in the North. Returning to Pennsylvania, he worked as a toolmaker until the call came to pastor a small church in Minnesota, where he was ordained in 1992.

Bob is self-employed as a cabinet maker. He and Doris also enjoy producing and marketing maple syrup, honey, and homemade jam. This gives them many opportunities to speak for the Lord in secular settings.

Bob began writing with a burden to testify to the relevancy of God's Word in everyday life and experience. His first two books, *Worth Remembering* and *Where Two Seas Met* (Christian Light Publications), are compilations of true short stories. *God Gave the Increase* is his first published longer work.

If you wish to contact Bob, you may email him at stauffer@paulbunyan.net or write to him in care of Christian Aid Ministries, P.O. Box 360, Berlin, Ohio 44610.

CHRISTIAN AID MINISTRIES

Christian Aid Ministries was founded in 1981 as a nonprofit, tax-exempt 501(c)(3) organization. Its primary purpose is to provide a trustworthy and efficient channel for Amish, Mennonite, and other conservative Anabaptist groups and individuals to minister to physical and spiritual needs around the world. This is in response to the command ". . . do good unto all men, especially unto them who are of the household of faith" (Galatians 6:10).

Each year, CAM supporters provide approximately 15 million pounds of food, clothing, medicines, seeds, Bibles, Bible story books, and other Christian literature for needy people. Most of the aid goes to orphans and Christian families. Supporters' funds also help clean up and rebuild for natural disaster victims, put up Gospel billboards in the U.S., support several church-planting efforts, operate two medical clinics, and provide resources for needy families to make their own living. CAM's main purposes for providing aid are to help and encourage God's people and bring the Gospel to a lost and dying world.

CAM has staff, warehouses, and distribution networks in Romania, Moldova, Ukraine, Haiti, Nicaragua, Liberia, and Israel. Aside from management, supervisory personnel, and bookkeeping operations, volunteers do most of the work at CAM locations. Each year, volunteers at our warehouses, field bases, DRS projects, and other locations donate over 200,000 hours of work.

CAM's ultimate purpose is to glorify God and help enlarge His kingdom. ". . . whatsoever ye do, do all to the glory of God" (1 Corinthians 10:31).

THE WAY TO GOD AND PEACE

We live in a world contaminated by sin. Sin is anything that goes against God's holy standards. When we do not follow the guidelines that God our Creator gave us, we are guilty of sin. Sin separates us from God, the source of life.

Since the time when the first man and woman, Adam and Eve, sinned in the Garden of Eden, sin has been universal. The Bible says that we all have "sinned and come short of the glory of God" (Romans 3:23). It also says that the natural consequence for that sin is eternal death, or punishment in an eternal hell: "Then when lust hath conceived, it bringeth forth sin: and sin, when it is finished, bringeth forth death" (James 1:15).

But we do not have to suffer eternal death in hell. God provided forgiveness for our sins through the death of His only Son, Jesus Christ. Because Jesus was perfect and without sin, He could die in our place. "For God so loved the world that he gave his only begotten Son, that whosoever believeth in him should not perish, but have everlasting life" (John 3:16).

A sacrifice is something given to benefit someone else. It costs the giver greatly. Jesus was God's sacrifice. Jesus' death takes away the penalty of sin for everyone who accepts this sacrifice and truly repents of their sins. To repent of sins means to be truly sorry for and turn away from the things we have done that have violated God's standards. (Acts 2:38; 3:19).

Jesus died, but He did not remain dead. After three days, God's Spirit miraculously raised Him to life again. God's Spirit does something similar in us. When we receive Jesus as our sacrifice and repent of our sins, our hearts are changed. We become spiritually alive! We develop new desires and attitudes (2 Corinthians 5:17). We begin to make choices that please God (1 John 3:9). If we do fail and commit sins, we can ask God for forgiveness. "If we confess our sins, he is faithful and just to forgive us our sins, and to cleanse us from all unrighteousness" (1 John 1:9).

Once our hearts have been changed, we want to continue growing spiritually. We will be happy to let Jesus be the Master of our lives and will want to become more like Him. To do this, we must meditate on God's Word and commune with God in prayer. We will testify to others of this change by being baptized and sharing the good news of God's victory over sin and death. Fellowship with a faithful group of believers will strengthen our walk with God (1 John 1:7).